THE TWO-WAY STRATEGY

By: O. Yahal

The Two-Way Strategy

1

A Guide to Knowing the Right Business to Start and Manage Successfully

---

[1] Nianzishe Biashara Gani Yahal?

Table of Contents

Contents

How to Read This Book

This book is an essential guide that promises to help you decide which type of business you can start and run successfully. It is designed for business-minded individuals who wish to, start a business or expand their business knowledge. I strongly recommend that you read the entire book, even if you have a weak background in business studies. If you need help to read the whole book, focus on specific sections that will provide you with the most valuable content. Read it in several sessions, take notes, and try to find something in real life that you can relate to what you've learned. By changing your mindset and unlearning everything you already know about business, you can follow this guide effectively and decide which business to start. This book will give you the knowledge and tools you need to succeed in your business endeavors. Now that you know how to read the book, I wish you all the best and hope you enjoy reading it.

ACKNOWLEDGEMENT

Starting a business can be daunting, and writing a book about it may seem even more challenging. However, I am proud to say that I have accomplished both. As a first-time author, I am thrilled to have completed this unique project, which displays my expertise and represents a significant milestone in my life. I understand that mistakes can happen, and if you come across any errors or mistakes in this book, I apologize in advance and ask for your forgiveness. I promise to do a better job in the 2nd edition and my subsequent books.

The idea of writing this book initially came to me as a joke. Still, as I heard countless stories of people struggling to find the right business to start or run effectively, I realized the importance of sharing my knowledge and experience. I was concerned about the alarming rate of businesses opening and closing, and I wanted to help others avoid making the same mistakes.

In writing this book, I aimed to achieve two primary objectives. Firstly, to help aspiring entrepreneurs avoid common pitfalls and make informed decisions when starting a business.

Secondly, help someone avoid starting a business because of the following: *have 100k……. ``, `` Business xy has much money…….``, ``Business xy has faster/ quick/good return on investment…….``, ``I want to own as business…. ``* and the most common one ` `*I* *want something to keep me busy……* ``. By the end of this book, I hope you will have a much more apparent, straightforward, realistic, and practical reason to start whichever business you have decided to start or the one you have already started.

If you want to start a business and ensure a positive return on investment in the shortest time possible, this guidebook is precisely what you need. It offers valuable insights into the most profitable business ventures. It is relevant to anyone considering starting a business, facing challenges in their current business, or simply curious about the latest industry trends.

Starting a business is one of the best decisions you can make, offering over 20 benefits to you as an entrepreneur, your community, and the government. However, using the right formula to ensure success is crucial, or you'll regret your decision. This guidebook is the perfect resource to help you achieve your goals, and it's a must-read for anyone serious about starting or growing a business. And let me be clear: while the journey to creating this guidebook was personal, it wouldn't have been possible without the support of a dedicated team. I would like to express my special thanks and gratitude to the following people:

- ✓ To my mother, who at the time of writing this book had already gone to be with the Lord 20 years ago. Mom, thank you for playing your role so well despite our short time together. I love you.

- ✓ To all the men whom I have interacted with, thank you;
- ✓ To all the women whom I have interacted with, wow!
- ✓ To Mr. Thomas Nudi, whom I will always consider my mentor and friend, Thank you, Senior; I am grateful. GAA;
- ✓ To My mom, Mrs. Bahati Gatere, you are a darling. You practically raised me during my early campus life. Thank you, Ero Kamano.
- ✓ To all my former employers, thank you.

Dedication

I dedicate this work to my son Yahal Jnr. and my late friend Jane Nyokabi.

~To Yahal Jnr., make the days count, don`t count the days. You are free to give up on everything and anyone but never give up on yourself.

~To Jane, I wish we had more time together. I love you. I will miss you for a very long time. Thank you for our time together.

Forward

To you who are reading this book,

With great pleasure and enthusiasm, I introduce to you "The Two-Way Strategy" by Yahal Otieno a comprehensive guide to navigating the intricate landscape of choosing the right business to start or managing an already existing business. In a world brimming with endless possibilities, embarking on the entrepreneurial journey requires more than just ambition; it demands strategic thinking, insight, and a keen understanding of the intricate web that is the business world.

Yahal Otieno is not only a long-time friend but also a brother who inspires me with his passion for business and leadership. He is a seasoned entrepreneur and brings to you a roadmap that transcends the conventional approach to business selection. In his book "The Two-Way Strategy," Otieno masterfully combines practical wisdom with a strategic framework that empowers aspiring entrepreneurs to make informed decisions about the type of business they should venture into.

This book is not just another manual on entrepreneurship; it is a beacon of light for those at the crossroads of possibilities. Otieno delves deep into the intricacies of business selection, guiding you through a thoughtful process that considers your passion and the market dynamics, trends, and the ever-evolving demands of the local, regional, and global economy.

"The Two-Way Strategy" is not a one-size-fits-all solution; instead, it serves as a personalized guide, helping you uncover your unique strengths and align them with the opportunities in the business landscape. Otieno's insights are derived from his experiences and a thorough understanding of successful business models across various industries.

Whether you are a budding entrepreneur or someone contemplating a shift in your career path, this book will empower you to make choices that resonate with your goals and values. Otieno's Two Way Strategy is not just a formula; it's a mindset that encourages you to embrace the dynamic nature of entrepreneurship and to see every challenge as an opportunity for growth. As you embark on this journey with Yahal Otieno, may you find inspiration, clarity, and the confidence to take the plunge into the world of entrepreneurship armed with the knowledge and strategic insights provided in "The Two-Way Strategy."

Here's to your success and to the exciting ventures that lie ahead!

GAA

All the best!!

Thomas Nudi | Social Entrepreneur | Philanthropist | Leadership Missionary
Founder & CEO
Nudi Empire Foundation

1.0 PART 1: INTRODUCTION

1.1 CHAPTER ONE

Vision

S tarting a business is good, but beginning with the right vision is the best. As an entrepreneur, you must ask yourself why you want to start a business. [2]The stronger the WHY the easier the HOW. Your why must be so good and fulfilling that you are willing and ready to risk everything to achieve it. Most entrepreneurs are more focused on the financial gain a business can give them rather than the value the business

Why Do You Want to Start a Business?

they are starting will give the targeted consumers. A business that doesn't offer any value to customers will fail no matter how hard the entrepreneur works or how well he or she is resourced. A good business is as good as the solution it's providing to its targeted consumers.

Financial gain as the primary motivating factor for starting a business is not bad but what I must tell you, is that it's not sustainable, and funny enough you might end up being very

---

[2] The more valid your reason is to your target clients, the easier it will be to start

frustrated by such motivation. That is why as an entrepreneur you must have a very good reason why you are starting a business. The reason for starting a business in most cases is and should be your vision. The vision makes you disciplined and focus. A good vision should be more focused on the target consumers rather than on you as an entrepreneur.

Starting a business may seem easy, but managing one is another story altogether. Therefore, it's crucial to lay a strong foundation for your business. Regardless of the type of business you're starting or working at, it's essential to have a clear goal, objective, or vision written down. Doing this will help you avoid making terrible mistakes. Understanding why you're starting/managing a business is crucial, and having a well-defined goal/vision is vital. The better and clearer the goal/vision is, the easier it is to start/manage the business successfully.

It is crucial to ensure that you clearly understand your vision for starting your business every day. This vision will be your ultimate guide and source of strength during your entrepreneurial journey. You will need a steady supply of guidance and strength to achieve this. As my first advice, I suggest you [3]write your vision/goals, and objectives on a clean page with clear and good handwriting. This

---

[3] Most serious institutions like schools have their vision, mission and core values clearly displayed for all to see, I am insisting that you do the same.

way, anyone, including you and your employees, can easily read and understand it.

In writing your vision/goals/objectives, ensure that the vision is [4]SSMART. That is to say, ensure that your vision is: Simple, Specific, Measurable, Attainable, Realistic, and Has a clear time frame of how long it will take. For example, in the next five years, you can envision being, the largest and most affordable retailer of fresh farm produce within Nairobi, Kenya. This vision is SSMART, for it is straightforward and specific; the business person wants to start a new farm produce retail business in Nairobi. The vision is measurable and attainable; the business person wants to be a large retailer, not small or medium, and yes, when a business is large, it can offer more affordable prices to its consumers for it has relatively more control over their factors of production, which are a significant contributor in price determination. Lastly, the vision is realistic, and the time frame of 5 years is authentic and transparent.

In the above vision, the business person will still have to define the following in detail.

---

[4] A smart Vision will make you more discipline, thus improving your chances of succeeding.

- Large – is it in terms of overall revenue, physical size of the business, and number of customers the company will be serving, or is it in terms of the stock the industry will have?
- Affordable products specifically, considering that there are products that the lower the price, the lower the demand. The entrepreneur will have to specify that his products are affordable in respect to what?
- Fresh farm Produce particularly fresh farm produce. A list of all the farm products the entrepreneur wishes to sell should be made.
- Time – 5 years from what time or at which point, as from the business star or when the company has already broken even.

The entrepreneur will have a very SSMART vision and a clear step-by-step guide by carefully going through the above.

The following are some characteristics of a good vision to help you develop a better vision. A good vision;

i.   .Is admirable

ii.   Can be broken down into smaller simple steps/actions

iii.   Solves an apparent problem

iv.   Can be measured.

v.   Has the either financial or social benefit

vi.   Is simple to understand and easy to remember

vii.   Is scary at first but gets friendly with time

viii.   Is Sustainable

A clear vision is crucial for any business to succeed, whether you are already managing or planning to start a new one. Note that a vision that is long-term and spans at least five years is highly recommended. It's worth noting that a vision can evolve, and new milestones can be added to it. Once a vision is achieved, the business owner can choose to end the business, start a new one, or come up with a new vision.

If a business fails to achieve its vision, the owner can still choose to end it, start a new one, or continue with it differently. However, seeking professional advice before making such a decision is wise. For SMEs, if the business is still struggling after three years or has yet to achieve at least half its vision/goals/objectives, it's essential to seek professional help.

Mission and Co values

Having a clear vision is essential for any business. Once you have a vision, the next step is to define a mission. The mission is a set of daily activities or actions the business will perform to achieve its vision. Additionally, the values of the company, or how the business operates, are also critical. These values, known as co-values, should align with the mission and vision of the business.

It is essential to outline the daily, weekly, monthly, and even yearly activities that will be performed to achieve the vision. These activities should be SMART (Specific, Measurable, Achievable, Relevant, and Time-bound). All business members/ employees and other shareholders should know the mission and understand why it was chosen. The mission of the company should be derived directly from its vision. Failure to clearly define the daily, weekly, and monthly activities will make it impossible for the business to achieve its vision, leading to failure.

Business Name

Just the same way you do have a name, a [5]business must have a name as well. The name must be in clear display for all to see, thus you must ensure that you do the naming the right way. Once you have settled on the vision, mission, and the co values of your business, the next important thing is to ensure that you have the right name for your business. Most entrepreneurs take this process for granted and they end up coming up with funny names for their businesses, a mistake that can affect their businesses directly in most cases. A business name sets the basis for your business brand image. Considering that every business is a brand, by default, thus a good business name is mandatory.

A not-so-serious business name will automatically make your brand to be seen as a not-so-serious brand. Also, a business name that seems too serious will make your brand appear too serious

---

[5] Never start a Business without a name, this is my commandment number 3

thus driving away certain types of clients. It is therefore very important that a business has the right name that will make the brand be perceived in a way that benefits the business.

A business name needs to be generated based on these factors or using the following strategies:

1. **The solution the business is providing or the problem the business is trying to address**: If your business is solving a very unique problem that either affects a huge group of people or a small group of people, you should use this strategy to name your business.

2. **The name of the entrepreneur**; especially if the entrepreneur will be the one either producing the goods/services or if they will be the one involved directly in the customer service {selling the goods or directly offering the service(s)}. This naming approach is mainly recommended in service-oriented businesses.

   For example, if you are planning to open a pedicure shop and you will be doing the pedicure, you should name your business after you. This naming strategy is mainly encouraged especially if you are so good at what you do. If you will mainly be using employees to interact with the clients, I will discourage you from using this strategy.

3. **A word or a name that either represents or is familiar to the target audience.** Using this strategy makes the target

audience easily identify with your business. For example, if you are a dental or eye doctor, it is highly advisable to use this naming strategy Note that for some sensitive types of business this might not be the best strategy. For example, if you are a doctor who has specialized in treating STDs, you should use this strategy to name your business.

4. **Location of your business;** your business is located at a strategic location within an area, you are highly advisable to name your business after the location.

   For instance, if your business is located at a well-known junction of a town, it will be highly advisable that you name your business after that famous junction, i.e., Banana Junction Butchery. I will highly recommend you use this naming strategy for community-based/oriented businesses such as health clinics, etc.

5. **Be creative but don`t copy or hijack a trending name or word.** When coming up with the name of your business and all the 1st 4 strategies do not work for you are allowed to come up with a creative name for your business. The creative name can be an acronym, a combination of two names, or even a short form of a name.

   I strongly discourage the naming of a business after seasonal trending words, phrases, and names. The danger of doing that is that it makes you look uncreative and with time after the word, name, and phrase stop to trend your business name will lose taste. Doing this also causes your business to lose authenticity and true identity.

I would highly recommend you use this naming strategy in a cosmopolitan environment or in an area dominated by youths and youths being your main target audience/customers.

Characteristics of a good business name

1. Simple and Easy to remember.
2. Easy to read and pronounce.
3. Represents what your business is doing where your business is located or the solution your business is providing.
4. Has a meaning either to you or to your target audience.
5. Has no language barrier especially if you are operating in a cosmopolitan area.
6. Not too long.
7. Not too serious or too unserious.
8. Not abusive.
9. Not similar to another business name.

Business Location

Your business should and must have a location, the [6]location can either be physical, virtual, or both. Selecting the right business location is a critical decision that can significantly impact the success and sustainability of a venture. The choice of a business location involves a complex interplay of various factors that extend beyond mere geography. It encompasses considerations such as target market proximity, accessibility, local regulations, and infrastructure.

The strategic placement of a business establishes its presence within a community, allowing it to tap into a specific customer base and cater to the unique needs of the local market. Moreover, the chosen location influences operational efficiency, affecting everything from supply chain coordination to workforce availability. In today's interconnected global economy, businesses must navigate a dynamic landscape where digital and physical presence converge. As such, a comprehensive understanding of the business environment, coupled with a nuanced approach to location selection, is essential for companies aiming to thrive in an ever-evolving marketplace.

---

[6] In this Digital age, you must a virtual location, i.e. a website or an official social media page

Characteristics of a good business location

Selecting an ideal business location is a multifaceted process that goes beyond traditional brick-and-mortar considerations, encompassing both physical and virtual dimensions. This document delves into the key characteristics of an optimal business location, exploring the constructive collaboration between the physical and virtual aspects to provide a comprehensive guide for businesses navigating the complex terrain of location selection.

I. Characteristics of a good Physical Business Location:

1. Accessibility and Visibility:
   - Proximity to major transportation hubs, highways, and public transit.
   - Visibility and ease of access for customers, ensuring a steady flow of foot traffic.

2. Demographics and Target Market:
   - Understanding the local population demographics and aligning them with the target market.
   - Analyzing consumer behavior patterns to tailor products or services to meet local preferences.

3. Competitive Landscape:
   - Conducting a thorough analysis of competitors in the area.
   - Identifying niches or gaps in the market that can be leveraged for a competitive advantage.

4. Infrastructure and Amenities:

- Availability of essential utilities and robust infrastructure.
- Access to amenities such as restaurants, banks, and recreational spaces for employees and customers.

5. Regulatory Environment:
   - Comprehending local zoning laws, permits, and regulations.
   - Ensuring compliance with environmental standards and other legal requirements.

II. Characteristics of a good Virtual Business Location:

1. Online Presence:
   - Robust and user-friendly website to facilitate online transactions.
   - Effective use of e-commerce platforms and digital marketing strategies.

2. Cybersecurity Measures:
   - Implementing strong cybersecurity protocols to protect customer data.
   - Ensuring a secure online transaction environment for both the business and its customers.

3. Digital Infrastructure:
   - Reliable and high-speed internet connectivity.
   - Seamless integration with cloud services for scalability and flexibility.

4. Global Accessibility:

- Adapting the business model for a global audience.
- Utilizing virtual collaboration tools for remote work and international partnerships.

5. User Experience:

- Optimizing the website and digital interfaces for a positive user experience.
- Embracing innovative technologies like augmented reality or virtual reality for enhanced engagement.

Factors to consider when setting up a physical business location

Setting up a physical business location is a pivotal step in realizing entrepreneurial aspirations. Beyond the attraction of a prime spot, numerous factors play a crucial role in determining the success and sustainability of a brick-and-mortar location.

1. **Location, Location, Location**: The adage holds— the choice of location is paramount. Consider the target market, foot traffic, and accessibility. Proximity to transportation hubs, complementary businesses, and a visible storefront can significantly impact a business's reach and visibility.

2. **Market Analysis**: Conducting a thorough market analysis is indispensable. Understanding the demographics, consumer behavior, and competitors in the area will guide strategic decisions. This analysis enables businesses to tailor their offerings to meet local demands effectively.

3. **Costs and Budgeting:** Setting up a physical location involves various costs beyond the lease or purchase price. Consider renovation expenses, utilities, permits, and staffing costs. Developing a detailed budget ensures that financial resources are allocated judiciously.

4. **Zoning and Regulations**: Comprehending local zoning laws and regulations is imperative. Ensure that the chosen location aligns with the intended business activities and meets legal requirements. Obtaining the necessary permits and licenses is vital to avoid legal complications down the line.

5. **Foot Traffic and Accessibility:** The volume of foot traffic and ease of accessibility directly influence a business's success. Evaluate the surrounding infrastructure, parking availability, and public transportation options. A location with high footfall can contribute significantly to brand exposure and sales.

6. **Competition Analysis**: Assessing the competitive landscape is crucial for differentiation. Identify competitors in the vicinity, understand their strengths and weaknesses, and determine how your business can offer unique value to the target audience.

7. **Infrastructure and Amenities**: Ensure that the chosen location has adequate infrastructure and essential amenities. Reliable utilities, proper waste disposal facilities, and proximity to necessary services like banks and post offices contribute to operational efficiency.

8. **Scalability and Future Growth**: Anticipate future business growth and assess whether the chosen location can accommodate expansion. Consider the scalability of the physical space and evaluate the potential for market growth in the surrounding area.

9. **Community Engagement:** Building a positive relationship with the local community is invaluable. Engage in community events, support local causes, and establish connections with neighboring businesses. A strong community rapport can enhance brand loyalty and foster a positive business environment.

10. **Technology Integration**: Embrace technology to streamline operations and enhance customer experience. Implementing modern point-of-sale systems, inventory management tools, and digital marketing strategies can contribute to operational efficiency and customer satisfaction.

Factors to consider when setting up a Virtual Business Location

1. **User-Centric Website Design**: Crafting a virtual storefront demands more than aesthetics—it requires a user-centric design. Prioritize responsive layouts, seamless navigation, and swift loading times to create an immersive and positive user experience that keeps visitors engaged.

2. **Mobile Optimization**: With the pervasive use of mobile devices, optimizing your virtual space for mobile platforms is non-negotiable. Stay aligned with Google's mobile-first indexing

paradigm to guarantee accessibility and flawless performance across a spectrum of mobile devices.

3. **E-Commerce Integration**: For businesses engaged in online transactions, a robust e-commerce platform is the cornerstone. Ensure secure payment gateways, streamline the checkout process, and provide transparent product information to instill trust and foster a high conversion rate.

4. **Cybersecurity Measures:** Safeguarding customer data is paramount in the virtual space. Employ cutting-edge cybersecurity protocols and stay vigilant against evolving cyber threats. Regularly update security systems to maintain a robust defense against potential risks.

5. **Search Engine Optimization (SEO):** Elevating online visibility is a continuous journey. Stay attuned to the latest SEO best practices, including strategic keyword optimization, high-quality content creation, and adapting to search engine algorithm updates to ensure a prominent position in search results.

6. **Data Privacy Compliance**: As data privacy concerns escalate globally, businesses must strictly adhere to data protection regulations. Stay informed about and comply with laws such as GDPR and CCPA, implementing measures to responsibly handle and protect customer data.

7. **Digital Marketing Strategies**: Develop and execute dynamic digital marketing strategies to drive traffic to your virtual location.

Leverage social media platforms, content marketing, and email campaigns to build brand awareness and foster meaningful engagement with the target audience.

8. **Adaptability to Emerging Technologies:** Embrace cutting-edge technologies to enhance the virtual experience. Stay abreast of trends like augmented reality, virtual reality, and voice search to provide innovative and immersive interactions, setting your virtual presence apart from the competition.

9. **Customer Support and Engagement**: Prioritize responsive customer support through various channels, including live chat, chatbots, and email assistance. Foster a sense of community and brand loyalty by actively engaging with customers through social media platforms.

10. **Analytics and Performance Monitoring**: Harness the power of analytics tools to monitor and optimize your virtual location's performance. Track website traffic, analyze user behavior, and measure conversion rates to gain valuable insights. Regularly refine strategies based on data-driven decisions to continually enhance the virtual customer experience

Considerations for Business Compliance

In your business operations, compliance with regulatory standards is not only a legal requirement but a crucial element for fostering trust, sustainability, and long-term success.

1. **Legal Compliance**:

- Local Regulations: - Adherence to local laws, zoning ordinances, and licensing requirements is fundamental. Understanding and complying with the legal framework of the specific region where a business operates is paramount.

- National Regulations: - Compliance with national laws, such as labor laws, taxation regulations, and industry-specific mandates, ensures a solid legal foundation. Staying abreast of changes in national legislation is crucial for avoiding legal pitfalls.

- International Compliance: - For businesses operating across borders, navigating international laws, trade agreements, and cultural nuances is imperative. Compliance with global standards and treaties prevents legal complications and enhances a company's reputation on the global stage.

2. **Ethical Considerations:**

- Corporate Social Responsibility (CSR): - Embracing CSR practices involves considering the environmental, social, and economic impacts of business operations. Companies need to align their strategies with ethical practices to contribute positively to the communities they serve.

- Anti-Corruption Measures: - Implementing robust anti-corruption policies ensures ethical business conduct. This involves preventing bribery, corruption, and unethical practices both within the organization and in its interactions with external stakeholders.

3. **Industry-Specific Regulations:**

- Health and Safety Standards: - Compliance with health and safety regulations is crucial for maintaining a secure working environment. Regular assessments and training programs ensure that businesses adhere to industry-specific safety standards.

- Financial Regulations: - Finance businesses must comply with stringent financial regulations to ensure transparency, accountability, and the protection of stakeholders. This includes compliance with accounting standards, anti-money laundering (AML) laws, and customer data protection regulations.

- Healthcare Compliance: - Healthcare-related businesses must navigate a complex web of regulations, including patient privacy laws (HIPAA), pharmaceutical regulations, and quality standards. Non-compliance can result in severe legal consequences.

4. **Data Protection and Privacy:**

- General Data Protection Regulation (GDPR): - For businesses handling customer data, compliance with GDPR is essential. This European regulation dictates how companies collect, process, and store personal data, ensuring individuals' privacy rights are protected.

- Cybersecurity Compliance: - Protecting sensitive data from cyber threats is paramount. Businesses need to implement robust cybersecurity measures, conduct regular audits, and stay compliant with data protection laws to mitigate the risk of data breaches.

5. **Employee Relations and Labor Laws**:

- Equal Employment Opportunity (EEO): - Ensuring fairness and preventing discrimination in the workplace is mandated by EEO laws. Businesses need to create policies and practices that promote diversity and equal opportunities for employees.

- Fair Labor Standards Act (FLSA): - Compliance with labor laws, such as minimum wage requirements and overtime regulations, is crucial. Understanding and implementing fair labor practices fosters positive employee relations and prevents legal disputes.

6. **Environmental Compliance:**

- Environmental Protection Laws: - Businesses must comply with environmental regulations to minimize their ecological footprint. This includes waste management practices, emissions controls, and sustainable resource usage.

Market Research

[7]Market research is a systematic and organized process of collecting, analyzing, interpreting, and disseminating information related to a specific market, industry, or business environment. Its primary purpose is to gain insights into the market dynamics, consumer behavior, and competitive landscape, enabling businesses to make informed decisions, develop effective strategies, and stay competitive in a dynamic marketplace.

Key Components of Market Research

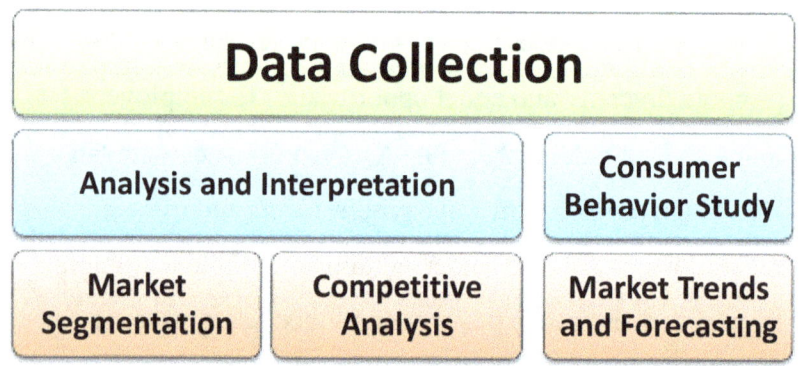

1. **Data Collection**: Primary Research: Involves the direct gathering of data from sources through methods like surveys, interviews, focus groups, and observations. Secondary Research: Utilizes existing data from sources such as industry reports,

---

[7] Market research is a continuous process/ activity that should be done at least once a year. It is the ultimate external litmus test for your business

government publications, academic journals, and market intelligence.

2. Analysis and Interpretation: This involves examining collected data to identify patterns, trends, correlations, and relevant insights. It also involves utilizing statistical methods, qualitative analysis, and data visualization techniques to extract meaningful information.

3. Market Segmentation: Dividing the target market into distinct segments based on characteristics such as demographics, psychographics, behavior, and geographic location. This helps in understanding specific consumer needs and tailoring strategies accordingly.

4. Competitive Analysis: Evaluating the strengths and weaknesses of competitors to identify opportunities and threats in the market. This helps in understanding market positioning, pricing strategies, and product offerings of competitors.

5. Consumer Behavior Study: Is examining how consumers make decisions, including factors influencing purchasing choices, preferences, and attitudes. This helps businesses tailor products, services, and marketing strategies to meet consumer needs.

6. Market Trends and Forecasting: Helps in identifying current and emerging trends that may impact the market. By forecasting future market conditions, it aids in strategic planning and decision-making.

Objectives of Market Research

1. Informed Decision-Making: Market research helps in providing decision-makers with accurate and timely information to support strategic choices.

2. Understanding Consumer Needs: Market research helps in gaining insights into customer preferences, expectations, and behavior to tailor products and services.

3. Risk Mitigation: Market research helps in identifying potential challenges, risks, and opportunities to proactively address market uncertainties.

4. Opportunity Identification: Market research helps in discovering new market opportunities and niches for business expansion and growth.

Applications of Market Research

1. Business Planning: Market research is integral to the formulation and refinement of business strategies, helping businesses stay relevant and competitive.

2. Marketing Strategy: Market research guides the development of effective marketing campaigns, advertising, and promotional activities.

3. Product Launch: Market research assists in understanding market readiness and optimizing product features and positioning.

4. Customer Satisfaction and Loyalty: Market research aids in assessing and improving customer satisfaction, loyalty, and retention strategies.

5. Investment and Financial Planning: Market research supports financial decision-making by providing insights into market conditions and potential returns on investment.

How to Conduct a Market Research

i. **Define Crystal-Clear Objectives**: The success of any market research endeavor starts with well-defined objectives. Articulate precisely what insights you aim to gain – whether it's understanding consumer behavior, gauging market trends, or evaluating competitive landscapes.

ii. **Methodology Tailored to Objectives:** Select a research methodology aligned with your goals. Whether quantitative or qualitative, employ surveys, interviews, focus groups, or data analytics, ensuring the chosen methods harmonize with your research objectives.

iii. **Precision in Target Audience Definition:** Identify and understand your target audience thoroughly. Factors such as demographics, psychographics, and geography should shape your audience definition, ensuring your research captures relevant insights.

iv. **Crafting a Thoughtful Survey/Questionnaire**: When using surveys, design questions that are clear, concise, and unbiased. A balanced mix of open-ended and closed-ended questions facilitates a more comprehensive understanding of consumer perspectives.

v.   **Meticulous Data Collection:** Execute your chosen methodology diligently to collect data. Whether through online surveys, interviews, or other means, maintain consistency and impartiality throughout the data collection process.

vi. **Rigorous Data Analysis:** Employ statistical tools and qualitative analysis methods to scrutinize your findings. Uncover patterns, correlations, and trends that will serve as the bedrock for strategic decision-making.

vii. **Transform Insights into Action**: The true value of market research lies in its ability to translate findings into actionable insights. Identify strategic directions and implement changes based on the substantiated data.

Benefits of Market Research

a) Precision in Decision-Making: Market research provides a data-driven foundation for decision-making, reducing uncertainties and enhancing the likelihood of successful outcomes.

b) Holistic Understanding of Consumer Needs: By delving into consumer preferences and needs, businesses can tailor their products or services to align seamlessly with market demands.

c) Proactive Opportunity and Threat Identification: Market research empowers businesses to identify emerging opportunities and potential threats, positioning them strategically in a competitive landscape.

d) Agile Risk Management: Anticipate shifts in the market and changing consumer behaviors to proactively mitigate risks and adapt to dynamic market conditions.

Factors Critical to Effective Market Research

a) Budgetary Considerations: Allocate resources judiciously, ensuring that the financial investment in market research aligns with the depth and breadth of insights required.

b) Timely Insights: Align the research timeline with the urgency of information needed, choosing methodologies that balance thoroughness with expediency.

c) Competitor Analysis: Conduct a comprehensive analysis of the competitive landscape to ensure your research captures the full spectrum of market dynamics.

d) Ethical Research Practices: Uphold the highest ethical standards in data collection, respecting participant privacy and maintaining the integrity of the research process.

Hallmarks of a Good Market Research

Excellence in market research demands an unbiased and objective stance, free from preconceived notions that could compromise the integrity of the findings. Secondly, employing a robust research design and methodology is important to ensure the reliability and validity of the results obtained.

Another hallmark of good market research is its capacity to provide actionable insights that drive strategic decision-making within the organization. Fourthly is to recognize market research as a continuous, adaptive process that evolves alongside changes in the market environment and consumer behavior.

Lastly, good market research presents research findings in a clear, accessible manner, fostering effective communication across all levels of the organization and facilitating informed decision-making.

SWOT Analysis

SWOT analysis is a strategic planning tool used to assess and evaluate the internal Strengths and Weaknesses of an organization, as well as the external Opportunities and Threats it faces. The acronym "[8]SWOT" stands for Strengths, Weaknesses, Opportunities, and Threats, encapsulating a systematic approach to

---

[8] SWOT analysis is a continuous activity that should be done at least twice a year. It is the ultimate internal litmus test for your business.

understanding both the internal capabilities and limitations of a business or project and the external factors that may impact its performance.

Components of SWOT Analysis

a) **Strengths**: These are the internal factors that give an organization a competitive advantage. E.gs include unique capabilities, valuable resources, strong brand reputation, skilled workforce, or efficient processes.

b) **Weaknesses**: These are the internal factors that pose challenges or limitations to the organization. These can include deficiencies in resources, skill gaps, operational inefficiencies, or any other internal aspect hindering optimal performance.

c) **Opportunities**: These are the external factors in the environment that the organization can leverage for growth and success. Opportunities may arise from emerging market trends, technological advancements, changes in consumer behavior, or new partnerships.

d) **Threats**: These are the external factors that could potentially harm or impede the organization's success. Threats may include increased competition, economic downturns, regulatory changes, technological disruptions, or shifts in consumer preferences.

Purpose and Objectives of SWOT Analysis

a) Strategic Planning: SWOT analysis serves as a foundation for strategic planning, helping organizations align their objectives with their internal capabilities and the external environment.

b) Decision-Making: SWOT analysis Provides valuable insights for decision-makers to make informed choices by considering both internal strengths and weaknesses and external opportunities and threats.

c) Risk Management: SWOT analysis Aids in identifying and mitigating risks by assessing potential threats and weaknesses, allowing organizations to develop proactive strategies.

d) Performance Evaluation: SWOT analysis Facilitates a holistic evaluation of an organization's current position, enabling the identification of areas for improvement and optimization of strengths.

3D SWOT Analysis

a) Internal Assessment: Evaluate organizational strengths and weaknesses by analyzing factors such as resources, capabilities, processes, and performance metrics.

b) External Assessment: Identify external opportunities and threats by examining market trends, competitor activities, regulatory changes, and other external forces.

c) Integration: Synthesize internal and external findings to formulate strategic initiatives that capitalize on strengths, address weaknesses, exploit opportunities, and mitigate threats.

Applications of SWOT Analysis

a) Business Strategy: SWOT analysis is used in strategic planning to align organizational goals with internal capabilities and external factors.

b) Project Planning: SWOT analysis is applied to assess the viability and potential challenges of specific projects, guiding decision-making throughout their lifecycle.

c) Marketing Planning: SWOT analysis helps in developing effective marketing strategies by understanding market dynamics and identifying unique selling propositions.

d) Organizational Development: SWOT analysis is utilized in organizational development to foster continuous improvement and adaptability.

How to Conduct a good SWOT Analysis step by step:

a. Identify Strengths (S):

- Evaluate internal aspects that provide a competitive edge.

- Analyze unique skills, resources, and capabilities.

- Consider factors that contribute to brand equity.

b. Assess Weaknesses (W):

- Scrutinize internal factors that hinder optimal performance.

- Identify areas that require improvement in processes or resources.

- Reflect on any gaps in skills or capabilities.

c. Explore Opportunities (O):

- Look externally for potential avenues for growth and advancement.

- Consider emerging market trends, technological advancements, or untapped customer segments.

- Identify partnerships or collaborations that could be beneficial.

d. Evaluate Threats (T):

- Examine external factors that could pose challenges or risks.

- Consider market competition, regulatory changes, economic downturns, or technological disruptions.

- Anticipate potential obstacles to future growth.

e. Integration and Synthesis:

- Draw connections between internal strengths and external opportunities.

- Mitigate weaknesses by leveraging identified opportunities.

- Address threats by leveraging internal strengths or mitigating weaknesses.

Direct Benefits of SWOT Analysis:

a) Strategic Decision-Making: SWOT analysis provides a structured approach for decision-makers to align strategies with internal strengths and external opportunities.

b) Holistic Understanding of Business Positioning: SWOT analysis offers a comprehensive view of where the business stands about both internal and external factors.

c) Risk Mitigation: SWOT analysis enables proactive identification and mitigation of potential threats and weaknesses.

d) Resource Optimization: SWOT analysis facilitates the allocation of resources to areas with the highest potential for positive impact.

Factors Critical to Effective SWOT Analysis

a) Realism and Objectivity: Ensure a realistic assessment, avoiding overly optimistic or pessimistic viewpoints. Foster objectivity by seeking input from diverse perspectives within the organization.

b) Continuous Review: Recognize that business environments evolve; therefore, regularly update the SWOT analysis to reflect changing circumstances.

c) Data-Driven Analysis: Base conclusions on verifiable data rather than assumptions. Leverage key performance indicators (KPIs) to quantify strengths, weaknesses, opportunities, and threats.

d) Stakeholder Involvement: Involve key stakeholders to gather diverse insights and ensure a well-rounded analysis.

Hallmarks of an Effective SWOT Analysis

A successful SWOT analysis provides clear insights that lead to actionable strategies and initiatives. It encompasses a wide range of factors, including internal processes, market dynamics, and external influences. Thirdly it aligns with the overall strategic goals and vision of the business.

A good SWOT analysis successfully integrates SWOT findings into the business planning process, guiding decision-making at every level. Lastly, it should demonstrate the ability to adapt strategies based on changing internal and external conditions.

Random Quotes

❖ What you become when you go through a struggle is worth being proud of.

❖ Never make significant decisions when you are tired, but if you have to, decide to try again.

❖ Nobody knows who you are yet, even you; you don`t know who you are until you become, so become.

❖ Change with time, for change will happen.

1.2 CHAPTER TWO

WELCOME TO CLASS

In this chapter, I will briefly introduce business, particularly for those who have never taken a business class. It is essential to have a basic understanding of this subject before starting a business. If you have taken a business class before, you can treat this as a refresher course.

Business is a simple, engaging, and practical subject. I encourage you to have a positive attitude and approach it open-mindedly. The concepts covered in this book are basic and easy to understand, so there is no need to panic. If you are worried, remember that you can always refer back to this book as needed.

Business

Business is simply the activities carried out by an individual or an organization concerning providing goods and services to make a profit. Other scholars define it as the art and science of buying and selling goods and services between a willing buyer and a willing seller at a place of convenience for both parties, i.e., the market, along the road, in the house, on online platforms, etc.

Business Studies

Business Studies is the study of activities in and around the production and consumption of goods and services. I can also define it as the process of trying to understand the art and science of buying and selling between a willing buyer and a willing seller at a place of convenience for both parties. The person who buys goods or service(s) is known as a buyer/ consumer/ customer. Note that the buyer is the person who initially didn't have the goods or the service but eventually ends up with either the goods or the service(s). To get the goods or services, the buyer will either give the seller money or other goods or services in exchange. When a good or service is substituted with another good or service, that type of transaction is called ***Batter Trade.***

The person who sells goods or service(s) is known as a seller/service(s) or goods provider. The seller is the person who ends up losing possession of goods or services, although some services, like teaching, can`t be detached from the provider. In most cases, sellers gain money or other goods or service(s) in the event of a batter trade.

Other relevant terms that we can look at are:

- **Production,** which is the creation of goods and services or increasing their usefulness. If one is involved in producing goods and services, they will be referred to as a producer. Companies involved in the production of Iron sheets are good examples of producers. Manufacturers and processors fall under this category.

- **Distribution** is the movement of goods and services from the producer to the users/consumers/clients. People who distribute goods/services are referred to as distributors. Most logistics companies are distributors. The newspaper and bread vendors are a good example of distributors in Kenya.

- **Consumption** is the act of using the goods or services produced. Consumption is usually the ultimate goal of production. The people who use a good or service are known as consumers. Consumers can be individuals or other businesses.

Disciplines of Business Studies

Business studies have five main disciplines as follows:

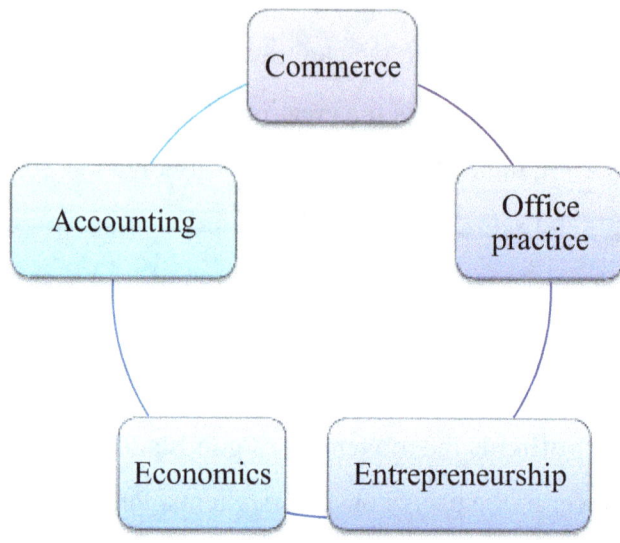

1: Disciplines of Business Studies

Pillars	Explanation	E.gs
Commerce	This is the study of trade and aids to trade.	E.gs of aids to deal with are banks.
Accounting	This is the systematic way of recording financial business activities, which is eventually used during decision-making.	Cash Book

Office practice	This refers to all the activities that are carried out in an office.	Printing, lamination, filling.
Economics	This studies how humans strive to satisfy their endless wants using the scarce/ limited available resources.	You are using $200 to buy food for your family.
Entrepreneurship	This study involved identifying a business opportunity and acquiring the necessary resources to successfully start and run a business.	I am starting a food joint near a university targeting the university students who are off full board option of accommodation.

Goods vs. Services

2: GoodsVsServices

Goods are tangible items for sale, i.e., they can be touched. On the other hand, services are efforts, activities, or acts/ actions done in exchange for money or other form of payment or reward. **Services** are intangible (cannot be touched or felt but can only be seen when they are done or offered.).

Goods	Services
Can be seen	It cannot be seen.
Can be touched	It cannot be touched.
Perishable/expire	Not perishable

Importance of Business

Any Business has several benefits. To enable you to understand its importance, I will give a breakdown of the said importance in the main categories as follows:

a) To The Economy

- Job creation: Businesses are a massive source of employment, thus reducing unemployment and promoting economic stability.
- Wealth creation: successful businesses generate profits and wealth, contributing to personal and corporate taxes and stimulating government revenue.
- Export-oriented businesses bring foreign exchange earnings, strengthening the country's balance of payments and enhancing economic resilience
- Business activities positively influence the gross domestic product (GDP) of a country

b) To the Consumers

- Businesses make a range of goods and services available to the consumers.
- Good business competition ensures fair pricing; thus, consumers can choose what they can afford.
- Enable customers to get the very best of customer service, for businesses work hard to ensure that they offer the best customer service to their customers.
- Ensures that customers always get quality and their rights are not violated since the businesses are bound by law to offer quality products and to protect the rights of the consumers.

c) To the Government

- Businesses enable the government to collect revenue when paying for sales and payroll taxes, etc.
- Help the government create employment opportunities.
- Contributes significantly to the stability of the economy for the government.

d) To the Business person or Entrepreneur.

- Enables the business person to fulfill their vision and passion.
- Creates job opportunities for the business person
- Enables the business person to be creative and innovative.
- Give the business person an opportunity to grow, considering that it's not easy to manage a business.

Home Trade

3: Trade

Trade is the buying and selling of goods and services. Home trade is the buying and selling of goods and services within the boundary of a given country. Home trade is further divided into Retail trade and Wholesale trade. The opposite of home trade is international trade or foreign trade, which is the buying and selling of goods and services beyond the boundaries of a country. This type of trade can be carried out between individuals or governments of different countries. International trade between two countries is called bilateral trade, while when many countries are involved, it is called Multinational trade.

International trade is divided into Export trade and Import trade. Export trade is selling goods and services from one country to another country, individuals in one country to another, or individuals across different countries. On the other hand, import is buying goods and services by one country or individual from another country or individual in another country.

Forms of Home Trade

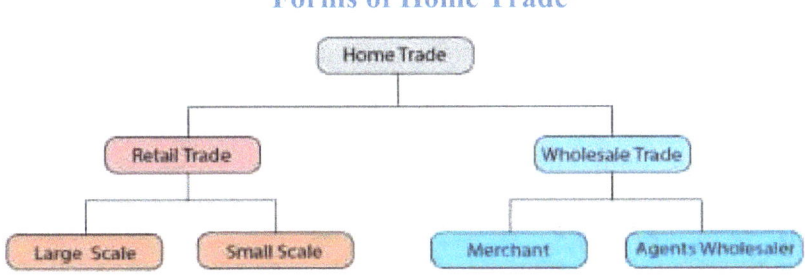

4: Home Trade

Home trade, a fundamental component of the broader economic landscape, encompasses various transactions involving buying and selling goods and services within a domestic market. This intricate web of commerce involves retailers and wholesalers, each playing distinct roles in facilitating the flow of products from producers to end consumers.

I. Retail Trade

Retail trade, the initial point of contact for consumers, is a dynamic sector that involves the acquisition of goods and subsequent sale to the final consumers. Retailers, from small-scale enterprises to large establishments, fulfill indispensable roles connecting producers, wholesalers, consumers, and government entities.

A. Small-Scale Retailers:

1. Kiosks: Small, standalone retail structures often found in busy public areas, offering convenience and accessibility to consumers.

2. Market Stalls: Fixed or temporary setups in markets where various vendors display and sell their goods to diverse customers.

3. Tied Shops: Retail outlets affiliated with a particular brand or manufacturer, emphasizing brand loyalty and exclusivity.

4. Single Shop Units: Independent stores that operate as standalone entities, serving local communities with a focused product range.

5. Mobile Vendors (e.g., hawkers): Flexible retailers who move from one location to another, providing convenience and adaptability in reaching diverse consumer groups.

B. Large-Scale Retailers:

1. Supermarkets: Expansive retail spaces offering various products, organized into aisles for easy customer navigation.

2. Chain Stores: Retail outlets that are part of a more extensive network, sharing a common brand identity and management structure.

3. Departmental Stores: Multi-level retail establishments, categorizing products into departments for a comprehensive shopping experience.

4. Hypermarkets: Large retail spaces combining elements of supermarkets and departmental stores, offering diverse products and services.

5. Mail Stores: Retailers that conduct transactions through mail orders, providing convenience to customers who prefer remote shopping.

II. Wholesale Trade

Wholesale trade involves the acquisition of goods and services in large quantities from producers and manufacturers, with the subsequent distribution to retailers in smaller quantities. This intermediary step is crucial in ensuring the efficient flow of products within the supply chain.

A. Types of Wholesalers

1. General Merchandise Wholesalers: Entities that deal with a broad range of products, catering to the diverse needs of retailers.

2. Regional Wholesalers: Wholesalers that operate within specific geographic regions, facilitating efficient distribution within localized markets.

3. Cash and Carry Wholesalers: Wholesalers that require customers to pay in cash at the time of purchase, promoting financial efficiency.

III. Terms of Payment: Payment terms in home trade are pivotal aspects that define the financial transactions between buyers and sellers. These terms can either be in cash or through deferred payment (credit), depending on the mutual agreement and the terms and conditions of the business.

A. Cash Payment: Cash transactions involve the immediate exchange of money for goods or services. This method is straightforward and ensures quick and secure transactions.

B. Deferred Payment (Credit Payment):

Deferred or credit payment allows buyers to make payments later, usually after a specified period. This arrangement provides flexibility but requires trust between the parties involved.

IV. Documents Used in Home Trade:

In the complex web of home trade transactions, various documents are crucial in formalizing and documenting the exchange of goods and services. These documents serve as tangible evidence of a business transaction and provide clarity to all parties involved.

A. Preliminary Documents:

1. Letter of Inquiry: A formal document from a prospective buyer requesting information about products or services.

2. Catalogue: A comprehensive document highlighting a seller's products or services, providing detailed information to potential buyers.

3. Quotation: A formal statement outlining the prices, terms, and conditions under which a seller is willing to provide goods or services.

4. Price List: A document detailing the prices of various products a seller offers, aiding buyers in making informed decisions.

B. **Transactional Documents:**

1. Local Purchase Order: A document issued by a buyer to formally request the purchase of goods or services from a seller.

2. Acknowledgment Note: A written confirmation from the seller acknowledging the buyer's receipt of an order or inquiry.

3. Packing Note: A document specifying the details of the packaging of goods, ensuring accurate and secure delivery.

4. Advice Note: A communication from the seller to the buyer, providing information about the dispatch of goods.

5. Delivery Note: A document accompanying delivered goods, serving as proof of receipt for the buyer.

6. Consignment Note: A document outlining the details of transporting goods, facilitating smooth coordination and tracking.

7. Invoice: A formal document issued by the seller to the buyer indicating the type, quantity, and price of the goods or services provided.

8. Pro forma Invoice: A preliminary invoice issued by the seller before the actual delivery of goods or services, providing a preview of the transaction.

9. Credit Note: A document issued by the seller to the buyer indicating a reduction in the amount payable for various reasons, such as returns or discounts.

10. Debit Note: A document issued by the seller to the buyer indicating an increase in the amount payable, often due to additional charges or adjustments.

11. Receipt: A formal acknowledgment of payment received by the seller from the buyer.

12. Cheque: A written order from a buyer to their bank to pay a specific amount to the seller.

Supply Chain

A supply chain is a dynamic and interconnected ecosystem that involves coordination, collaboration, and optimization of resources to deliver products or services efficiently, meeting customer demands while minimizing costs and maximizing value. It plays a critical role in the success and competitiveness of businesses in today's globalized and fast-paced markets. Supply Chain in simple terms is the study of how goods and services move from the initial/primary producer to the final consumer. Supply chain management as a profession involves trying to find the most efficient, reliable, and cost-effective way that goods and services can easily move from the primary producer to the final consumers.

Key components of a supply chain:

1. Supplier: The supply chain begins with suppliers who provide the raw materials, components, or services needed for the production of goods or services. Suppliers can range from local providers to international partners, depending on the nature of the product.

2. Manufacturer/Producer: Once the raw materials are procured, manufacturers or producers transform them into finished products through production processes. This stage involves the assembly, manufacturing, or creation of goods according to specific requirements and quality standards.

3. Distributor/Wholesaler: Distributors or wholesalers act as intermediaries between manufacturers and retailers. They purchase goods in large quantities and then distribute them to retailers. They play a crucial role in managing inventory and ensuring products are available when needed.

4. Retailer: Retailers are businesses that directly sell products to consumers. They can operate through various channels, including physical stores, e-commerce platforms, or a combination of both. Retailers play a significant role in marketing, promoting, and providing customer access to products.

5. Customer: The end of the supply chain is the customer, who purchases and consumes the final product or service. Customer feedback and demand patterns influence the entire supply chain, shaping production and distribution strategies.

6. Logistics and Transportation: Logistics involves the management of the physical flow of goods and information throughout the supply chain. Transportation ensures the movement of products from one point to another, using various modes like trucks, ships, planes, or trains.

7. Inventory Management: Efficient inventory management is crucial in maintaining the right balance between demand and supply. It involves tracking, ordering, storing, and managing the flow of goods to prevent overstocking or stockouts.

8. Information Flow: Information flows play a vital role in coordinating the activities of different supply chain partners. Technologies such as Enterprise Resource Planning (ERP) systems and data analytics facilitate real-time information sharing.

9. Supply Chain Visibility: Supply chain visibility refers to the ability to monitor and track products as they move through the supply chain. Visibility allows stakeholders to make informed decisions, enhance responsiveness, and improve overall efficiency.

10. Risk Management: Supply chain management includes assessing and mitigating risks that can disrupt the flow of goods or

services. Natural disasters, geopolitical issues, and market fluctuations are among the potential risks that businesses need to address.

Relevance of supply chain

For someone looking to start a business, understanding the concept of a supply chain is crucial as it directly impacts various aspects of business operations, cost management, and customer satisfaction. A deep understanding of supply chain management is a strategic advantage.

1. Cost Efficiency and Profitability: As a business owner, optimizing the supply chain can contribute to cost efficiency. Efficient sourcing of raw materials, streamlined manufacturing processes, and effective distribution channels help in minimizing expenses. A well-managed supply chain can enhance profitability by reducing production costs and ensuring that resources are utilized effectively.

2. Product Quality and Customer Satisfaction: Effective supply chain management ensures that quality raw materials are sourced, leading to better product quality. By managing inventory and logistics efficiently, entrepreneurs can provide timely deliveries, meet customer expectations, and foster satisfaction.

3. Market Competitiveness: Understanding supply chain dynamics allows entrepreneurs to stay competitive in the market. By

adopting efficient production and distribution practices, businesses can respond swiftly to market demands and outperform competitors.

4. Risk Mitigation and Resilience: Entrepreneurs face various risks, from supply chain disruptions to market uncertainties. An understanding of supply chain management helps in identifying potential risks and developing strategies to mitigate them. Building resilience into the supply chain ensures the business can adapt to unforeseen challenges and maintain continuity.

5. Start-Up Sustainability: For startups with limited resources, optimizing the supply chain is essential for sustainability. Efficient inventory management prevents overstocking or stockouts, avoiding unnecessary costs. Entrepreneurs can leverage technology to enhance supply chain visibility, enabling better decision-making and resource allocation.

6. Customer-Centric Approach: Entrepreneurs aiming for long-term success should prioritize a customer-centric approach. A well-managed supply chain allows businesses to respond to customer needs promptly. Effective communication with suppliers, manufacturers, and distributors ensures a seamless flow of information, contributing to a positive customer experience.

7. Adaptation to Market Trends: The market is dynamic, and entrepreneurs need to adapt quickly to changing trends. A flexible

supply chain allows for swift adjustments in production and distribution strategies based on market demands. Being attuned to market trends through supply chain visibility enables entrepreneurs to make informed decisions.

8. Technology Integration: Entrepreneurs can leverage technology to streamline supply chain processes. Implementing modern solutions such as inventory management systems and data analytics enhances efficiency and decision-making. Technology integration contributes to scalability, allowing startups to grow their operations seamlessly.

The following are examples of supply chains concerning home trade:

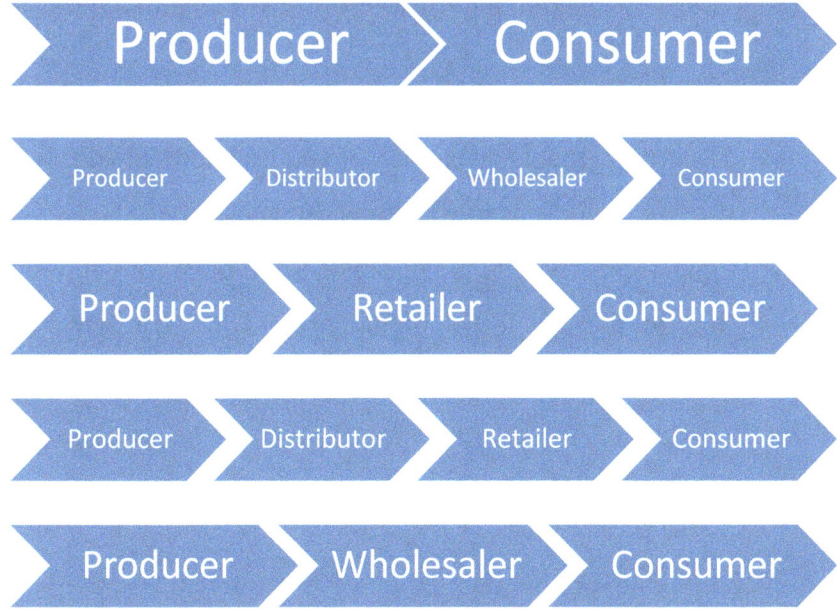

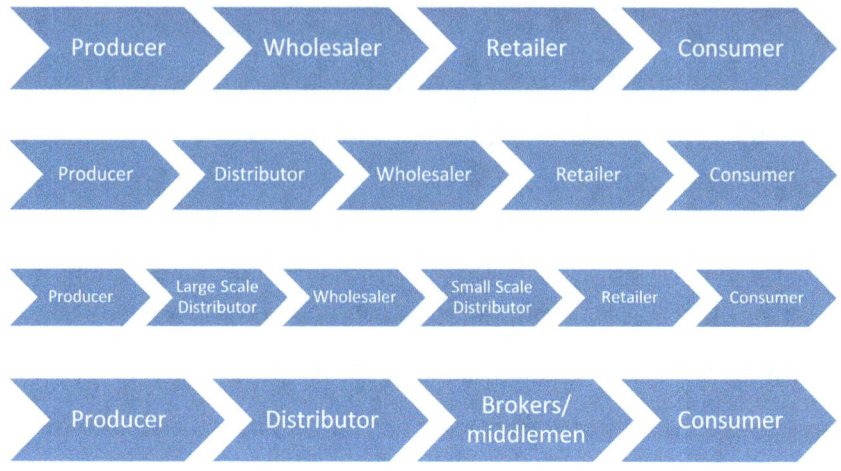

1.3 CHAPTER THREE

BEFORE YOU START

Before starting a business, it's essential to consider all possible aspects. The first step is to determine the specific idea for your business and how to come up with that idea. It would also be best to consider which personality traits you possess that will help you succeed as an entrepreneur.

Business Idea

A business idea is the conceptual foundation of a potential venture. It's the spark that ignites the entrepreneurial journey. This concept could be a product, service, or a combination of both that offers value to customers in a unique way. Business ideas often stem from identifying opportunities, solving problems, or capitalizing on trends in the market.

Business Idea Generation

Business idea generation is actively seeking and creating new concepts for a business. It involves a blend of creativity, research, and strategic thinking. This process can include brainstorming sessions, market analysis, and a deep dive into personal interests and skills. The goal is to develop innovative and viable business ideas that align with market needs and trends.

Business Gap Identification/Opportunity Identification

This step involves a more analytical approach. It's about identifying gaps or opportunities in the market where there is a demand for a product or service and a current need for more satisfactory solutions. This could be an underserved niche, an unmet need, or an area where existing offerings can be improved. The key is recognizing areas where your potential business could fill a void or provide a better alternative.

Developing a business idea involves generating concepts, whereas identifying a business gap entails finding the appropriate context or demand in the market for those concepts to prosper. The union of innovation and market exigency frequently results in prosperous ventures.

How To Identify a Business Gap

5:https://www.marketingdonut.co.uk/

Identifying a business gap is essential in the entrepreneurial journey, as it lays the foundation for creating a successful and sustainable business. The following points will help explain how to identify a business gap.

- Understand Industry Trends: Conduct thorough research on the industry you are interested in. Analyze current trends, emerging technologies, and shifts in consumer behavior. This will provide insights into potential gaps or unmet needs in the market.

- Competitor Analysis: Study existing competitors to identify areas where they may fall short or where customer dissatisfaction exists. Look for patterns in customer reviews, feedback, and complaints.

- Engage with Your Target Audience: Directly engage with your potential customers through surveys, interviews, or focus groups. Ask about their pain points, challenges, and unmet needs. Understanding customer perspectives is crucial in identifying gaps in the market.

- Feedback from Existing Products/Services: If you already have a product or service, gather feedback from existing customers. Understand what they like and dislike and any additional features or improvements they desire.

- Draw from Personal Experience: Consider your own experiences and identify areas where you've faced challenges or found solutions lacking. Your insights can lead to identifying a business gap that resonates with your needs and potentially those of others.

- Utilize Industry Expertise: If you have expertise in a particular industry or field, leverage that knowledge. Industry insiders often have a keen understanding of where the gaps and opportunities lie.

- Stay Informed about Technology: Keep abreast of emerging technologies and innovations within your industry. Technological advancements often create new possibilities and needs that businesses can address.

- Explore Cross-Industry Trends: Look beyond your industry and explore trends in other sectors. Sometimes, solutions applied in one industry can be adapted to fill gaps in another.

- Understand Your Target Audience: Conduct a detailed analysis of your target audience's demographics and psychographics. Understand their preferences, lifestyles, and values. This information can reveal gaps in the market that align with specific consumer needs.

- Identify Niche Markets: Look for underserved or overlooked niche markets within your target demographic. These segments may have unique needs not adequately addressed by existing products or services.

- Monitor Regulatory Changes: Changes in legislation or regulations can create new opportunities or gaps in the market. Stay informed about industry-specific regulations and anticipate how changes may impact consumer needs.

- Compliance Gaps: Identify areas where businesses may struggle to comply with new regulations. Developing solutions to facilitate compliance can fill a significant business gap.

- Attend Conferences and Trade Shows: Participate in industry conferences, trade shows, and networking events. These gatherings provide opportunities to connect with professionals, learn about industry challenges, and identify gaps your business can address.

- Build a Professional Network: Establish a network of industry professionals, entrepreneurs, and potential customers. Engage in conversations to gain insights into current market gaps and opportunities.

- Social Media Listening: Use social media platforms to listen actively to conversations within your industry. Monitor discussions, comments, and reviews to identify common pain points or unmet needs.

- Online Forums and Communities: Participate in online forums and communities relevant to your industry. Engage with discussions to understand the challenges individuals and businesses face and identify gaps where your venture could provide solutions.

- Assess Strengths, Weaknesses, Opportunities, and Threats: Conduct a SWOT analysis for your potential business idea. Identify the strengths and weaknesses of existing products or services in the market and the opportunities and threats that may indicate gaps.

- Develop Prototypes or Minimum Viable Products (MVPs): Create prototypes or MVPs to test your business concept in a real-world setting. Pilot testing allows you to gather feedback, identify shortcomings, and refine your offering before a full-scale launch.

- Iterative Improvement: Use feedback from pilot testing to iterate and improve your product or service. This iterative process ensures that your solution effectively addresses the identified gap.

- Consider Economic Trends: Economic changes can influence consumer behavior and needs. Analyze economic trends and assess how they might create or alter new gaps.

- Social Dynamics: Consider evolving social trends and cultural shifts. Changes in societal values and preferences can create opportunities for businesses to address emerging needs.

- Collaborate Across Functions: Involve professionals from diverse backgrounds, including marketing, sales, finance, and operations, in the gap identification process. Cross-functional collaboration brings varied perspectives, enriching the analysis and ensuring a comprehensive understanding of potential gaps.

- Stay Agile: The business landscape is dynamic, and gaps can shift over time. Establish a system for continuously monitoring market trends, consumer behaviors, and industry developments. Stay agile and be prepared to adapt your business model as needed.

- Customer Lifecycle Monitoring: Monitor the entire customer lifecycle—from awareness to purchase and post-purchase interactions. Identify points where customers may face challenges or where their needs are not adequately met.

- Utilize Data Analytics: Leverage data analytics tools to extract insights from large datasets. Analyzing customer behavior, market trends, and competitor performance through data analytics can unveil hidden gaps and opportunities.

- AI for Predictive Analysis: Explore using artificial intelligence for predictive analysis. AI algorithms can help predict future market trends and identify gaps based on historical data.

- Deep Dive into User Environments: Conduct ethnographic research by immersing yourself in your target audience's environments. Observe behaviors, challenges, and unmet needs firsthand to gain a nuanced understanding of potential gaps.

- Contextual Interviews: Conduct contextual interviews within the user's environment to elicit insights that may not emerge in traditional survey settings. This approach provides a deeper understanding of the user experience.
- Explore Global Markets: Consider a global perspective when identifying business gaps. Analyze trends and needs in different regions or countries. A gap in one market may present a significant opportunity in another.
- Cultural Sensitivity: Be culturally sensitive in your analysis. Understand how cultural nuances impact consumer behavior and preferences, ensuring your business solution aligns with diverse cultural contexts.
- Evaluate Environmental Impact: Assess the environmental sustainability of existing products or services in the market. Identify areas where businesses may fall short regarding ecological responsibility and explore eco-friendly alternatives as potential business gaps.
- Green Innovations: Innovate with a focus on environmental sustainability. Develop solutions that address consumer needs and contribute to sustainable practices, appealing to environmentally conscious consumers.
- Idea Mapping: Use idea mapping techniques to organize and connect various concepts visually. This visual representation

can help identify relationships between ideas and reveal potential gaps.

- Anticipate Future Scenarios: Engage in scenario planning to anticipate future scenarios that may impact your industry. Assess how different scenarios could create or alter new gaps, allowing you to position your business proactively.
- Risk Assessment: Consider potential risks and uncertainties in your analysis. Understanding the risks associated with a business gap helps you develop contingency plans and mitigate potential challenges.
- Review Legal Landscape: Examine the legal landscape related to your industry. Identify areas where legal constraints or ethical considerations may limit current offerings, leading to potential business gaps.
- Ethical Innovation: Explore opportunities for ethical innovation. Develop solutions that meet consumer needs and align with moral principles, appealing to a growing segment of socially conscious consumers.

Identifying a business gap is an ongoing process, and staying attuned to market changes is crucial. Combining multiple approaches, listening to the needs of your target audience, and maintaining a flexible mindset will enhance your ability to identify and capitalize on business gaps effectively. Additionally, the success of your business depends not only on identifying the gap but also on your ability to develop and deliver a solution that truly meets the needs of your target customers.

A Business Person

A business person is generally someone involved in the activities of running a business. This could include roles such as a manager, executive, or any individual contributing to the operation and administration of a company. Business people often focus on the day-to-day operations, management, and execution of existing business models. Their primary goal is to ensure the smooth functioning of the company, meet targets, and maintain profitability.

An Entrepreneur

An entrepreneur, on the other hand, is someone who not only runs a business but is also the driving force behind its creation. Entrepreneurs are characterized by their innovative and risk-taking nature. They identify opportunities, take calculated risks, and create something new. Entrepreneurs are often associated with the inception of a business, navigating uncertainties, and bringing new ideas to market. They are more likely to venture into unexplored territories, introducing novel products, services, or business models.

Understanding the entrepreneurial mindset

1. Embrace Uncertainty: Entrepreneurs thrive in uncertainty and see it as an opportunity for innovation. Embrace the unknown; view challenges as learning experiences, and be adaptable to change.

2. Risk-Taking and Resilience: Entrepreneurs are willing to take calculated risks and bounce back from failures. Develop a healthy relationship with risk, learn from setbacks, and cultivate resilience in the face of challenges.

3. Visionary Thinking: Entrepreneurs have a clear vision of what they want to achieve and set ambitious goals. Clearly define your business vision, set SMART goals, and constantly align actions with the bigger picture.

4. Adaptability and Flexibility: Entrepreneurs are adaptable to changing circumstances and are flexible in their approaches. Stay open to feedback, be willing to pivot when necessary, and embrace a mindset of continuous improvement.

5. Passion and Commitment: Entrepreneurs are driven by a passion for their ideas and are committed to seeing them through. Identify your passion, align your business with it, and maintain unwavering commitment through challenges.

6. Problem-Solving Orientation: Entrepreneurs see problems as opportunities to create solutions and add value. Develop a

problem-solving mindset; actively seek challenges and find innovative solutions.

7. Customer-Centric Focus: Entrepreneurs prioritize understanding and fulfilling customer needs. Put yourself in your customer's shoes, gather feedback, and consistently strive to exceed customer expectations.

8. Self-Confidence and Self-Belief: Entrepreneurs have confidence in their abilities and believe in the value of their ventures. Cultivate self-confidence through skill development, knowledge acquisition, and celebrating small wins.

9. Networking and Relationship Building: Entrepreneurs recognize the importance of building a network and fostering meaningful relationships. Network actively, seek mentorship, and value relationships as a key asset in your entrepreneurial journey.

10. Action-Oriented Mindset: Entrepreneurs prioritize taking action over perfection and are comfortable with experimentation. Overcome the fear of failure, take decisive actions, and learn from the outcomes.

11. Time Management and Prioritization: Entrepreneurs efficiently manage time, prioritize tasks, and focus on high-impact activities. Develop strong time management skills, prioritize tasks based on importance, and avoid unnecessary distractions.

12. Continuous Learning: Entrepreneurs have a thirst for knowledge and continuously seek opportunities for learning and growth. Read, attend workshops, engage in online courses, and actively seek knowledge in your industry and beyond.

13. Financial Literacy: Entrepreneurs understand the financial aspects of their business and make informed decisions. Invest time in understanding basic financial concepts, monitor cash flow, and make financially sound decisions.

14. Leadership Skills: Entrepreneurs exhibit strong leadership qualities, inspiring and guiding their teams. Develop leadership skills, communicate effectively, and foster a positive and collaborative work environment.

15. Gratitude and Mindfulness: Entrepreneurs appreciate the journey, celebrate successes, and practice mindfulness. Cultivate gratitude, acknowledge achievements, and take moments to reflect on the progress made.

Pros and Cons of Entrepreneurship

Pros

1. Independence and Autonomy: Entrepreneurs have the freedom to make decisions, set their own schedules, and chart the course for their business.

2. Creativity and Innovation: Entrepreneurs can bring their creative ideas to life, innovate in the market, and solve problems with unique solutions.

3. Potential for High Rewards: Successful entrepreneurs have the potential for significant financial rewards, both in terms of profits and personal wealth.

4. Learning and Personal Growth: Entrepreneurship provides continuous learning opportunities, promoting personal and professional growth.

5. Flexibility and Work-Life Balance: Entrepreneurs can create flexible work environments and potentially achieve a better work-life balance.

6. Building a Legacy: Entrepreneurs have the opportunity to leave a lasting legacy by creating and growing a successful business.

7. Control Over Decision-Making: Entrepreneurs have control over all aspects of their business, allowing for quick decision-making and adaptation.

8. Passion Pursuit Entrepreneurship often involves pursuing one's passion and turning it into a career.

Cons of Entrepreneurship

1. Financial Risk: Entrepreneurs face financial uncertainties, with the risk of losing personal savings or taking on debt.

2. Workload and Stress: Entrepreneurs often face long working hours and high levels of stress, especially in the early stages of the business.

3. Uncertainty and Instability: The business environment can be unpredictable, leading to uncertain cash flows and market fluctuations.

4. Responsibility and Pressure: Entrepreneurs carry significant responsibility, facing pressure from investors, customers, and employees.

5. Isolation: Entrepreneurship can be isolating, with entrepreneurs making critical decisions on their own and dealing with the weight of the business's success or failure.

6. Limited Resources: Startups often operate with limited resources, requiring entrepreneurs to wear multiple hats and juggle various roles.

7. Market Competition: The business landscape is competitive, and entrepreneurs must navigate challenges to stand out in the market.

8. Regulatory and Legal Challenges: Entrepreneurs must navigate complex legal and regulatory landscapes, which can be time-consuming and costly.

9. Work-Life Imbalance: Achieving a work-life balance can be challenging, especially during the initial stages of business development.

10. Failure and Rejection: Entrepreneurship comes with the risk of failure, and facing rejection is a part of the journey.

Factors of production

The factors of production are the resources required to produce goods and services. Traditionally here are four main factors of production:

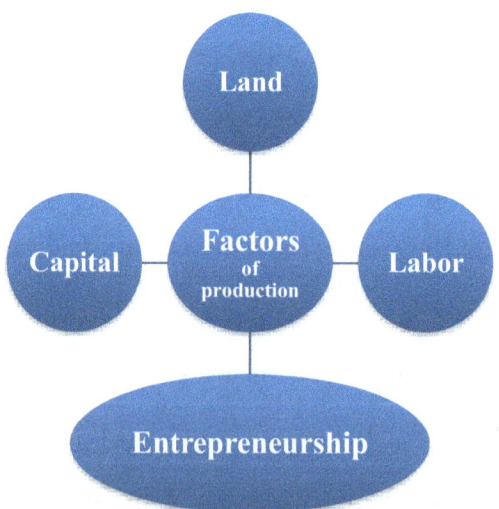

6: Factors of production

1. **Land**: This includes all natural resources used in production. It comprises not just the physical land itself but also the minerals, water, air, and other resources that come from or are on the land.

2. **Labor**: This refers to the human effort, both physical and mental, that goes into the production of goods and services. It encompasses the skills, knowledge, and abilities of the workforce.

3. **Capital**: In economics, capital doesn't just mean money. It includes all artificial resources used in the production process. This can range from tools and machinery to buildings and infrastructure.

4. **Entrepreneurship**: This is the factor that ties everything together. Entrepreneurs take the initiative to combine the other factors of production. They combine land, labor, and capital to create a product or service. Entrepreneurship involves risk-taking, innovation, and seeing and seizing opportunities.

Some modern economists also add a fifth factor: technology or information. Technology plays a significant role in production in today's increasingly digital and interconnected world. In a nutshell, land, labor, capital, and entrepreneurship are the classic factors of production that contribute to the creation of goods and services.

Hallmarks of a Good Business

The hallmark of a commendable business lies in its adherence to fundamental principles that contribute to its success and positive impact on society. Below are essential characteristics that define a good business:

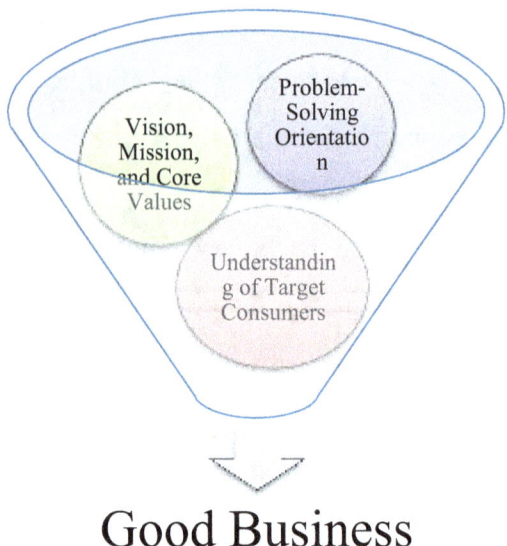

Good Business

7: Hallmarks of a good business

1. Vision, Mission, and Core Values: A reputable business should articulate a clear vision, mission, and core values as guiding principles. These foundational elements provide a sense of purpose and direction, shaping the company's identity and fostering stakeholder alignment.

2. Problem-Solving Orientation: An effective business addresses a distinct and tangible problem. By identifying and solving specific challenges, the business not only meets the needs of its target audience but also establishes itself as a valuable and purpose-driven entity in the market.

3. Understanding of Target Consumers: A successful business demonstrates a profound understanding of its target consumers. This involves defining a specific consumer demographic and tailoring products or services to meet their preferences, ensuring a more personalized and practical approach to addressing their needs.

4. Sustainability and Environmental Responsibility: A responsible business embraces sustainability practices and environmental consciousness. By adopting eco-friendly measures, such as minimizing carbon footprint and promoting responsible sourcing, the business contributes positively to the community and the planet.

5. Ethical Conduct: A good business is characterized by ethical conduct that prioritizes the well-being of its consumers. This includes avoiding actions that could harm consumers financially, physically, or otherwise. Upholding high ethical standards builds trust and credibility with the target audience.

6. Market Understanding: An astute business comprehensively understands the market in which it operates. This involves staying informed about industry trends, competitors, and consumer behavior. With this knowledge, the business can make informed decisions and remain competitive in a dynamic marketplace.

7. Flexibility and Adaptability: Flexibility is a crucial attribute of a successful business. The ability to adapt to changes in the

market, technological advancements, or shifts in consumer preferences ensures that the company remains resilient and responsive to evolving conditions. Flexibility allows for quick adjustments and innovation to stay ahead of the curve.

Pillars of a Successful Business

8: Pillars of a Successful Business

1. **Proper Market Research**: Identify distinct market segments and target audiences based on demographics, psychographics, and behavioral factors. For instance, a fitness app might target individuals interested in home workouts or personalized training programs. An entrepreneur needs to monitor market trends continuously to anticipate shifts in consumer preferences. Staying ahead of artificial intelligence or sustainable tech trends in the technology sector can inform product development. Each business needs to understand the market in which it operates. A

good understanding of the market makes the company understand the market's needs quickly.

2. **Knowing your Consumers:** A business needs to Collect and analyze demographic information such as age, gender, income, and location. This helps tailor marketing messages and product features to specific groups. Understanding their customers' age and income level is crucial for a high-end skincare brand. Explore customer behaviors, such as purchasing frequency and brand loyalty. In the gaming industry, understanding the gaming habits of your audience can guide game development and marketing efforts. The better a business understands its customers, the easier the company's running will be.

3. **Staying ahead of competition**: Evaluate competitors' strengths, weaknesses, opportunities, and threats. This analysis informs your own strategic decisions. Understanding competitors' features, pricing, and marketing strategies helps position your product effectively in the smartphone market. Continuously Keep tabs on competitors' innovations to identify gaps in the market. If a rival in the fashion industry introduces sustainable practices, it might prompt your brand to explore eco-friendly initiatives.

A business with aggressive competitors can benefit by constantly being challenged to be innovative and continually striving to offer its clients the best customer services, thus allowing the company to get and retain more clients. Having competitors as a business gives you a unique opportunity to show your clients how different your business is from the rest, which will likely make a business more successful if executed perfectly.

Any business with competitors should always avoid copying them at all costs. Still, if they have to copy their competitors, they should do so innovatively, bigger, and better. I must clarify that there are some essential industry standard things that you are free to do even if your competitor has already done them.

4. **Practicing modest Financial Accounting**: Financial accounting remains the main reason for the failure of most businesses. This is mainly contributed by poor bookkeeping practices, a mixture of personal finances, poor financial discipline, no financial strategy, and using the business finances to care for irrelevant individual needs.

Develop a detailed budget outlining expected income and expenses. This is crucial for financial planning. A restaurant, for example, needs to budget for ingredients carefully, staff salaries, and overhead costs. As a business owner, monitor cash flow to ensure the business has enough liquidity to cover day-to-day operations. Managing inventory levels is essential in manufacturing to prevent cash flow bottlenecks.

5. **Sound Human Resource Management**: Assess candidates for skills and cultural fit within the organization. In a creative agency, hiring individuals who align with the company's innovative and

collaborative culture fosters a positive work environment. Invest in ongoing training and development programs to enhance employees' skills. In the tech sector, providing coding workshops or certifications supports continuous learning.

6. **Keeping tabs on the Trends in Business:** To stay caught up, Stay abreast of emerging technologies relevant to your industry. Adopting blockchain technology or AI-driven solutions could enhance services and remain competitive in finance. Understand shifts in consumer behaviors, such as the rise of online shopping. A retail business might adapt by strengthening its e-commerce platform and optimizing the online shopping experience.

Random Quotes

❖ Good things will never be handed to you, even though prayers and fasting

❖ You need some courage in your life, even if it's wavering

2.0 PART 2

THE STRATEGIES

9: Credit to:https//:BenefitsCanada.com

The strategies shared in this book are designed to guide you toward the right trajectory for your business and to provide you with realistic expectations. Having clear and realistic goals for your business will significantly improve your chances of survival. If you investigate thousands of businesses, you will find out that unrealistic expectation is the main reason for 90% of new businesses fail.

In this book, I aim to provide truthful and factual expectations, so that you can make an informed decision about starting a business. I look forward to reducing the number of failed companies within the first few months. Each business having a specific vision, mission, objectives, and core values is necessary when starting a business. Starting a business should be an intentional activity, and you should never start a business just for the sake of it. Keep your expectations in check and strive to do everything possible to make your business successful.

Something to think about

Have you ever wondered why a business that seems very promising, done by someone who seems to know what they are doing ends up failing, while a simple business done by someone who seems to be doing trial and error ends up doing well and surviving for years? A practical example is a business that was opened near where I stay, that opened and closed within two weeks despite the entrepreneur having adequate capital and the know-how of how to run a business. Contrary to that, I know of a simple businessman who has been roasting maize for the last 15 years, and through that business, he has managed to take his children to school, buy land, and build a good home.

From the above e.gs, some of the questions that we must ask ourselves are:

1. What is the businessman roasting maize doing right and what did the businessman who closed within two weeks do wrong?

2. Does the success of a business depend on how good the idea is or can any idea succeed?

3. Does the educational background of an entrepreneur determine the success of a business?

4. Does the financial capability of an entrepreneur matter in the success of a business?

5. What is the motivating factor that is keeping the businessman who has been roasting maize for the last 5 years

6. Why did the businessman who closed within two weeks not start roasting maize as well?

I hope you have answers to these questions already but if don`t, then by the end of this book I know that you will have the answers.

Lessons from the Book: Blue Ocean Strategy

After reading The Blue Ocean Strategy, authored by professors W. Chan Kim and Renée Mauborgne, I agreed with their innovative approach to starting a business, which significantly diverges from traditional competitive thinking. The book offers a new framework that motivates entrepreneurs to create new market spaces or "blue oceans" instead of competing in overcrowded and competitive "red oceans."

The Blue Ocean Strategy challenges the conventional belief that success comes from outperforming rivals within existing industry boundaries. Instead, it advocates for entrepreneurs to break free from the constraints of competition and redefine the market landscape. The metaphorical red ocean symbolizes industries saturated with fierce competition, where companies fight for a share of the existing market. In contrast, the blue ocean signifies untapped market space, where opportunities for growth and innovation abound.

One of the fundamental principles of the Blue Ocean Strategy is the simultaneous pursuit of differentiation and low cost. Traditionally, businesses faced a trade-off between offering unique products and services at a higher price or providing standardized offerings at a lower cost. However, the Blue Ocean Strategy encourages businesses to challenge this trade-off by creating a unique value proposition that attracts a broader audience while maintaining cost efficiency.

Businesses must undergo a systematic process to implement the Blue Ocean Strategy successfully. This involves the formulation of a strategy canvas, a visual representation that outlines a company's current competitive factors and strategic focus. By critically evaluating these factors, businesses can identify areas of overemphasis and underperformance, paving the way for strategic innovation.

The Blue Ocean Strategy also introduces the concept of the Four Actions Framework, which consists of eliminating, reducing, raising, and creating factors within an industry. This framework prompts businesses to rethink their value propositions by removing or lowering factors the industry has long competed on, raising some aspects to new levels, and creating entirely new dimensions of value.

A notable aspect of the Blue Ocean Strategy is creating uncontested market space. This involves exploring opportunities beyond the boundaries of existing industries, often by redefining the industry itself. Cirque du Soleil serves as a prime example of this strategy in action. By combining elements of traditional circuses with theater and fine arts, Cirque du Soleil carved out a blue ocean in the entertainment industry, attracting a new audience and eliminating the need for animals, a staple in traditional circuses.

The Blue Ocean Strategy is not just for large corporations but equally applies to startups and small businesses. By encouraging a shift from a competitive mindset to a creative and innovative one, enterprises of all sizes can find their unique value propositions and tap into unexplored markets.

The Blue Ocean Strategy is a paradigm-shifting approach that challenges businesses to escape the red oceans of competition and venture into the uncharted territories of blue oceans. Companies can create new market spaces by differentiating and lowering costs, fostering innovation and sustained growth. Businesses can systematically navigate this transformative journey through strategic frameworks like the strategy canvas and the Four Actions Framework, unlocking unprecedented opportunities and securing a competitive edge in the ever-evolving business landscape.

From the Blue Ocean strategy, we can say that blue ocean markets are a "push" type of business, while red ocean markets are a "pull" type of business. One may be scared of starting a red ocean type of business. However, I hope you can choose the right business type that suits you by understanding properly each strategy. Also, if you are running a red ocean type of business, don't panic. Instead, find a way to use strategic frameworks like the strategy canvas and the Four Actions Framework to transform your business systematically, thus unlocking unprecedented opportunities and securing a competitive edge in the business world.

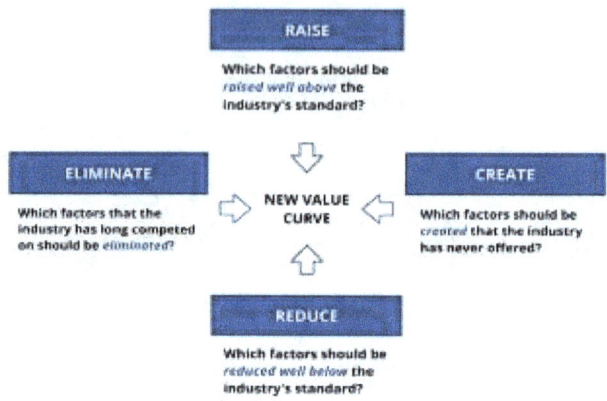

10: Four Actions Framework:

2.1 CHAPTER ONE

PULL STRATEGY

You

Pull strategy businesses are entities that entrepreneurs are drawn to for various reasons like potential profit, market demand, prestige, or their positive role in the community. These ventures captivate the attention of individuals, enticing them to embark on the entrepreneurial journey. The ease of entry into these businesses is attributed to the fact that they have been successfully established and operated by others. However, the key to success lies in introducing innovative approaches or doing better than others.

An intriguing aspect of pull strategy businesses is the inherent customer attraction. Customers actively seek out these businesses due to their essential goods or services. The relationship between the business and its clientele becomes symbiotic. However, the paradox lies in these businesses' intense competition, contributing to a saturated market. Entrepreneurs need to establish and maintain a competitive advantage to thrive.

Managing a pull strategy business can be challenging and complex. Therefore, a strategic approach is essential. One piece of fundamental advice is to acquire the necessary knowledge and training to oversee the business effectively. Alternatively, hiring professionals with expertise in relevant areas can provide invaluable support. Starting such a venture without the requisite knowledge and skills can lead to significant losses and frustration, potentially culminating in the decision to cease operations.

Initially, the start of a pull strategy business is marked by enthusiasm and joy, driven by the fascination of profit and societal impact, creating a positive atmosphere. However, this optimism might be short-lived when challenges arise. Stiff competition, demanding customers, unreliable suppliers, stringent government regulations, management difficulties, unforeseen market changes, and economic slowdowns are formidable obstacles that can overshadow the initial excitement. At this point, the entrepreneur may regret starting the business and may even consider ending it.

Pull strategy businesses typically present themselves as opportunities to fill a gap in the market or as sound investments worthy of financial commitment. While this proposition holds, the importance of due diligence must be considered. I highly recommend that you conduct thorough market research and analysis before starting this type of business to avoid encountering the challenges and problems I have mentioned earlier. The consequences of inadequate due diligence are stark, often resulting in business failures within a relatively short time frame.

A comprehensive entrepreneur's checklist of essential elements should come to the forefront regarding due diligence. Ensuring that the business meets at least three hallmarks of a good business is a foundational step. These hallmarks include factors such as solving a specific problem, sustainability, and having a clearly defined target customer. Adhering to these criteria positions the business for growth within two years or less, marking a critical phase in its development.

General Characteristics of Pull Strategy

Pull strategy type of businesses has the following characteristics;

- You mainly get into them due to the apparent availability of a gap in the market. For example, an area with a good population of young children but doesn't have a baby shop specializing in selling baby products is a suitable gap between the area and the market.

- Mainly doesn't have many barriers to entry. Compared to other types of businesses, the barriers present in these types of companies are negligible and, in most cases, can be solved easily.

- There is ready demand, but only if you have the proper supply. For example, there is a constant demand for fresh farm produce; if you can develop a business that produces or supplies such products, you will never lack demand.

- In most cases, they have good short-term return/profit/interest, especially when done correctly. For example, you open a shoe-selling business today, and after a sale of one show on the same day, you can make a profit.

- It's open to diversify/ mix more than one type of business into one, i.e., You can be into the food business but still offer mobile money services, or you can be doing a shoe repair business and still be able to provide rental caretaker services to landlords.

- Such a business has a well-defined/ specific working hour, i.e., 8 am to 5 pm or 6 am to 9 pm. This is mainly due to the behavioral patterns of the clients.

- One must have some basic skills to manage it effectively. For example, you must have basic or good arithmetic skills to be a shopkeeper. You need to have teaching skills to be a teacher.

Advantages and disadvantages of the pull Strategy:

Pull strategy types of businesses have advantages and disadvantages. Some of the advantages are as follows:

- Easy to start and run, especially with the proper knowledge and skills.
- Has the potential to reward you as an entrepreneur awesomely, especially when you do everything right.
- Profit can be realized within a short period.
- It's easy to identify a gap in the market.

The following are some of the disadvantages of pull strategy type of businesses:

- When there is poor financial management, losses and, eventually, failure can be achieved quickly.
- The more the business grows, the more difficult it becomes to manage; thus, the proprietor must acquire new skills to manage the business constantly.
- Have numerous competitions because everyone wants a share of the profit.
- Can make losses even after a long period of making huge profits.

- They can easily be affected negatively by numerous external factors.

How to use Pull Strategy to your advantage

The following are how you as an entrepreneur can strategically use this approach to your advantage:

- **Identify Profitable Niches**: Pull strategy businesses often attract entrepreneurs because of their profitability. Identify niche markets within the industry that are particularly lucrative. Conduct market research to understand where the demand and the competition are relatively low. Tailor your offerings to cater to these needs, creating a competitive advantage.

- **Leverage Brand Prestige**: Businesses with a pull strategy often have a level of prestige or recognition. Build and leverage your brand. Invest in creating a solid brand identity that communicates trust, quality, and reliability. A well-established brand attracts customers and contributes to customer loyalty.

- **Understand Market Demand**: Pull strategy businesses thrive on existing market demand. Conduct thorough market research to understand current and future market demands. Anticipate trends and align your offerings with the evolving needs of your target audience. Stay agile and responsive to changes in consumer preferences.

- **Community Engagement:** Pull strategy businesses often play a significant role in the community. Actively engage with the community. Participate in local events, support community initiatives, and build strong relationships. A positive impact on the community enhances your brand reputation and fosters customer loyalty.

- **Easy Market Entry:** Pull strategy businesses are relatively easy to start. Capitalize on the ease of market entry by focusing on quick and efficient startup processes. Develop a lean business model, utilize technology, and streamline operations to enter the market swiftly and cost-effectively.

- **Competitive Advantage:** Entrepreneurs must establish a competitive advantage due to competition. Differentiate your business from competitors. This could be through superior customer service, innovative product features, or unique value propositions. Identify what sets your business apart and make it a focal point of your marketing strategy.

- **Continuous Training and Skill Development:** Knowledge and skills are crucial for long-term success. Invest in continuous training and skill development. Stay updated on industry trends, emerging technologies, and best practices. This ensures that you remain ahead of the curve and can adapt to changes in the market environment.

- **Hire Professionals:** Entrepreneurs may lack specific skills; hiring professionals can fill the gaps. If there are areas where you lack expertise, consider hiring professionals. This could be in areas such as marketing, finance, or operations. A skilled team enhances the overall capabilities of the business.

- **Build Customer Relationships:** Pull strategy businesses often have customers actively seeking them out. Focus on building solid relationships with customers. Implement customer loyalty programs, gather feedback, and prioritize customer satisfaction. A loyal customer base not only ensures repeat business but also serves as an advocate for your brand.

- **Strategic Marketing Campaigns:** Marketing is crucial in a pull strategy to attract customers. Develop strategic marketing campaigns to display the value of your products or services. Utilize both traditional and digital marketing channels to reach a wider audience. Highlight critical benefits and address pain points to attract potential customers.

- **Monitor Market Changes**: Awareness of market changes is essential for long-term success. Implement a robust monitoring system for market changes. Regularly assess customer preferences, competitor activities, and external factors impacting the industry. Adapt your strategies accordingly to stay relevant.

- **Due Diligence and Research:** Due diligence is crucial for avoiding potential challenges. Prioritize thorough due diligence before starting the business. Research market conditions, competition, and potential challenges. Ensure your business aligns with the hallmarks of a good company, addressing specific problems sustainably.

- **Focus on Sustainability**: Sustainable businesses will likely experience long-term success. Ensure your business model is sustainable. Consider environmental, social, and economic sustainability in your operations. This aligns with modern consumer preferences and positions your business as a responsible and forward-thinking entity.

- **Invest in Innovation**: Pull strategy businesses can benefit from innovation. Stay innovative in your products, services, or processes. Embrace new technologies and trends that can give your business an edge. Innovation keeps your offerings fresh and exciting for customers.

- **Customer-Centric Approach**: Customer satisfaction is paramount in a pull strategy. Adopt a customer-centric approach. Listen to customer feedback, address their needs, and continuously improve your offerings based on their preferences. A satisfied customer is likelier to become a loyal advocate for your brand.

- **Anticipate and Manage Challenges**: Challenges are inevitable; anticipating and managing them is critical. Develop contingency plans for potential challenges. Whether it's increased competition, regulation changes, or economic shifts, having a proactive strategy to navigate challenges ensures resilience and long-term viability.

Examples of businesses that use a pull strategy

The following well-known businesses all used the pull strategy when they wanted to start their businesses.

i. All the supermarkets, i.e., Naivas, Khetias, Cheanshelf, etc.

ii. All the local and city clubs, bars, and restaurants, i.e., Mulberry Project at the Alchemist, K1 Klub House, Black Diamond, Club Cubano, Safari Bar, Santana Club/ bar, Skylux Lounge, Kool and the Gang, etc.

iii. All the beauty parlors and beauty/ cosmetics shops, i.e., / Bestlady cosmetics, superior beauty store, etc.

iv. All the retail and wholesale shops around you, i.e., Rafiki general store/shop, blessed available shop, blue kiosk, Mama Ian kiosk, etc.

v. All the food joints, hotels, motels, and restaurants around you, i.e., Nya Thiru Motel, Kwa Wanjeri Hotel, Kafetogo Hotel, Lazarus Hotel, etc.

vi. All the farmers you know

vii. All the players in the transport industry, i.e., Kenya Airways, Kenya Railways Authority, Kenya Bus, Likana Matatu Sacco, Pipeline boda boda riders' associations, etc.

viii. All the suppliers you know about

ix. Most of the manufacturers and processors

x. Most consultancy agencies and the list goes on and on.

Dynamics of the Strategy

In the vast business world, the pull strategy type of businesses is characterized by fierce competition, limited growth opportunities, and a constant struggle to gain market share within existing industry boundaries.

A pull strategy business aims to outdo competitors through aggressive marketing, constant product innovation, or strategic maneuvers. This often leads to price wars as companies try to gain an edge, resulting in squeezed profit margins and a shift in focus from value creation to cost-cutting.

However, this strategy tends to reach a point of saturation where growth becomes a formidable challenge. The market becomes crowded with players, leaving little room for new opportunities. This results in businesses offering similar products and services, making differentiation increasingly tricky.

In a pull strategy business, businesses retain existing customers rather than find new ones. This often means that products and services become commoditized to meet the expectations of a familiar audience. Rather than introducing groundbreaking products, businesses tend to make incremental improvements to existing products, emphasizing stability over transformation.

While technological advancements are present in the pull strategy, businesses focus on enhancing existing products, services, or processes. This approach limits the potential for disruptive change within the industry. Enterprises invest in incremental advancements to gain a competitive edge, but these improvements often fall within the boundaries set by industry norms, resulting in a lack of genuinely transformative innovations.

As competitors vie for the same pool of customers, product offerings and services tend to converge. This makes it challenging for consumers to distinguish between businesses with similar offerings. The strategies followed by companies within the pull strategy become increasingly homogeneous, leading to a need for more strategic diversity in the market.

Acquiring new customers in a pull strategy business can be expensive. Companies must invest significantly in marketing and advertising to differentiate themselves, driving up costs and putting additional pressure on profitability. With most potential customers already captured by existing players, businesses in the pull strategy face significant challenges in expanding their customer base, making it an uphill battle.

Understanding these dynamics is crucial for businesses operating in a pull strategy. It highlights the inherent challenges associated with competition in saturated markets and underscores the need for a strategic shift to transcend these limitations.

Random Quotes

- ❖ The Harder the battle, the sweeter the victory
  - ❖ Indecision is the thief of opportunity.
- ❖ You better try and fail rather than fail to try.

2.2 CHAPTER TWO

PUSH STRATEGY

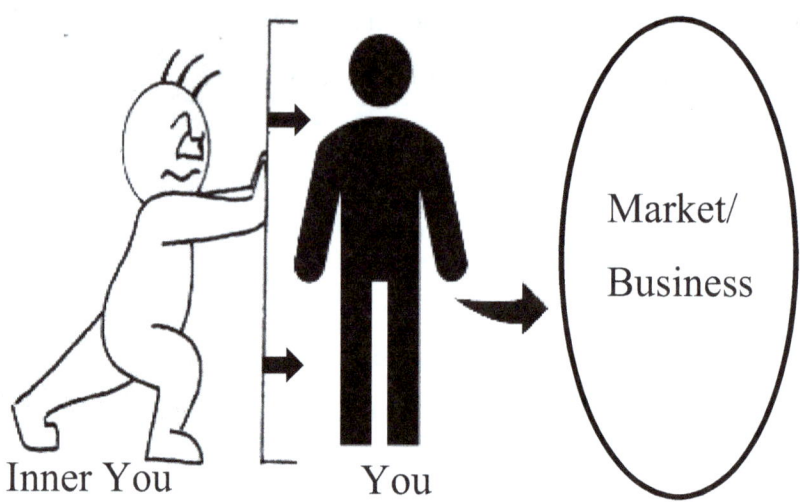

Inner You   You   Market/ Business

The push Strategy in entrepreneurship refers to the internal drive that motivates individuals to start a business. This innate push sets Push Strategy businesses apart from other business models initiated based on identified market gaps or perceived opportunities. In Push Strategy, entrepreneurs feel a magnetic pull toward a specific business idea or innovation, which continues to influence them until the business becomes a reality.

Push Strategy businesses offer entrepreneurs a high degree of autonomy regarding training requirements. Unlike other business models that require specialized training or industry experience, Push Strategy ventures often align with the natural skills and inclinations of the entrepreneur. This implies that individuals often feel equipped with the essential skills to embark on the chosen business endeavor without formal training.

Push Strategy businesses often involve pioneering endeavors, which contribute to their innovativeness and position them as trailblazers in their respective industries. In the early stages of a Push Strategy business, there is often a relative lack of competition due to the uniqueness and novelty associated with such ventures. This presents a favorable environment for entrepreneurs, allowing them to establish a foothold in the market with less immediate competition. The foundation for success can be laid during this critical phase, allowing the business to flourish.

Push Strategy businesses have a notable advantage in facing fewer regulatory constraints, especially in the early stages. This is because there are no established norms or precedents for these ventures. However, this lack of regulation can be both a blessing and a curse. Entrepreneurs have more freedom to operate, but they also have a greater responsibility to ensure that their business practices are ethical and legal.

In a Push Strategy business, entrepreneurs must actively seek out clients, customers, or consumers instead of waiting for demand to arise. This requires a proactive approach to identifying and engaging potential clients, which involves profoundly understanding the target audience. Entrepreneurs can directly connect with their clientele by customizing their products or services to meet their intended market's specific needs, preferences, and desires. This personalized approach creates a niche market and fosters customer loyalty, which is critical for long-term success.

Entrepreneurs embarking on a Push Strategy business must prioritize the customization of their offerings to align with the needs and wants of their target audience. However, this entrepreneurial model also poses challenges that individuals must navigate as their business progresses. These challenges include the need for continuous innovation, managing evolving market dynamics, and staying ahead of emerging trends.

General Characteristics of Push Strategy

Push strategy businesses are unique businesses with unique characteristics as follows:

- Sometimes, they are very difficult to start.
- They don't have significant competitors, especially during the early days; actually, they usually have a few indirect competitors
- They are mainly regarded as innovations or inventions

- Sometimes, they need many resources to start, but sometimes it doesn`t need much.
- They usually don't have ready demand; instead, they have hidden demand.
- There are no standard working hours; an entrepreneur can work for fewer or very long hours for days without rest.
- The entrepreneur has to convince people that the business can make money actively.
- Usually, they don't generate profit immediately; it can take up to 15 years before they start to make a profit.

Advantages and disadvantages of the push Strategy

Push strategy businesses have the following advantages:

- Once they start making a profit, they are unlikely to make losses
- They usually have a tremendously satisfying vision, more significant than money.
- Managing such a business becomes easy with time, for the more the business grows, the more the vision becomes clear to the proprietor
- Have the potential to change how many things are done normally

Just like any other strategy, the push strategy also has several disadvantages, as follows:

- Take time before the entrepreneur starts to enjoy profit.
- Its actualization usually looks impossible; thus, most people get discouraged or take a long time before starting.
- Getting funds is very difficult.
- Being a personal internal push type of business, its failure is usually very devastating, and in most cases, some entrepreneurs take their lives or lose complete direction in life.
- The entrepreneur has to do much hard work for long hours and days.

How to use Push Strategy to your advantage

Push strategy, as discussed, involves a solid internal calling or push to start a business, often driven by passion and innovation; here is how you as an entrepreneur can leverage this strategy to your advantage:

- **Follow Your Passion**: The inherent push or calling indicates a deep passion for the business idea. This passion can be a driving force, keeping the entrepreneur motivated and committed despite challenges. Channel your passion into your business. Use it to fuel creativity, resilience, and a genuine connection with your venture. Customers are often drawn to products or services that reflect the authentic enthusiasm of the entrepreneur.

- **Utilize Inherent Skills**: The belief that special training may not be necessary suggests that the entrepreneur already possesses the skills needed for the business. Identify and leverage your existing skills. This can accelerate the startup process and reduce the need for extensive training. Additionally, consider continuous learning to enhance and adapt your skills as the business evolves.

- **Embrace Innovation**: Push strategy businesses are often associated with innovation and novelty. Embrace your innovative ideas and approach. Use this advantage to differentiate your business in the market. Highlight the unique aspects of your products or services to attract early adopters and create a distinct brand identity.

- **Early Mover Advantage**: Push strategy businesses are described as having less competition, especially in the initial stages. Capitalize on being an early mover. Establish a strong presence in the market before competitors catch up. Focus on building brand recognition and customer loyalty during this initial period.

- **Adaptability and Flexibility:** Less regulation implies a degree of flexibility for push strategy businesses. Use this flexibility to your advantage. Be adaptive to market changes, customer feedback, and emerging trends. This agility allows you to refine your offerings based on real-time insights, giving you a competitive edge.

- **Customer-Centric Approach**: The push strategy emphasizes customizing products/services to fulfill customer needs. Prioritize understanding your customers. Conduct market research, gather feedback, and tailor your offerings based on customer preferences. A customer-centric approach enhances satisfaction and fosters brand loyalty.

- **Storytelling and Brand Narrative**: The internal push or Push can be a powerful storytelling element. Share your entrepreneurial journey as part of your brand narrative. Communicate the passion and inspiration behind your business. Storytelling creates a human connection with customers and can be a compelling marketing tool.

- **Network and Collaborate:** Networking is essential for entrepreneurs; your internal push may attract like-minded individuals. Build a network of collaborators, mentors, or partners who share your passion. Collaborative efforts can amplify your impact and provide valuable support. Networking also opens doors to potential customers and investors.

- **Continuous Improvement:** The persistent push implies a commitment to continuous improvement. Embrace a culture of constant learning and improvement. Regularly assess customer feedback, market trends, and internal processes. Adapt and evolve your business model to stay relevant and competitive.

- **Create a Compelling Brand Story**: The internal pressure to start the business can be a compelling element in your brand story. Craft a narrative that reflects the journey of how your company came to be. Share the challenges, inspirations, and milestones that led to its creation. A compelling brand story resonates with customers on an emotional level.

- **Strategic Marketing and Positioning:** Less competition in the initial stages allows for strategic marketing and positioning. Develop a clear marketing strategy to position your business uniquely. Highlight the innovative aspects, and use targeted marketing channels to reach your early adopters. Establish a solid online presence to maximize visibility.

- **Stay True to Your Vision:** The internal push often aligns with a strong entrepreneurial vision. Stay true to your vision even in the face of challenges. Your unwavering commitment can inspire confidence in customers and stakeholders. Consistency in delivering your brand promise builds trust over time.

Examples of businesses that used push strategy

As much as the push strategy type of business might seem very difficult to start, several successful businesses have used this strategy; the following are some examples:

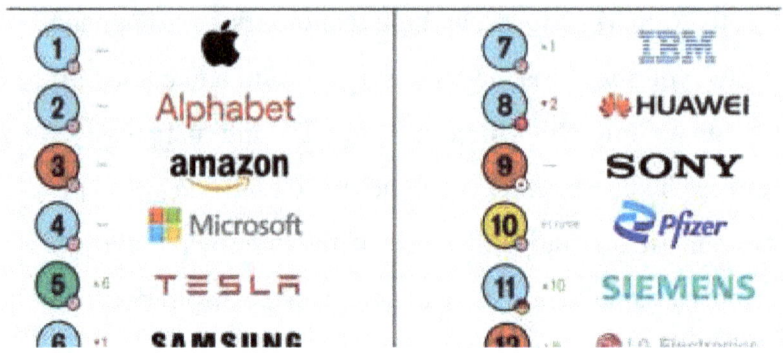

11:https://www.visualcapitalist.com

i. **Microsoft** was founded in 1975, and its headquarters is in Redmond, Washington, USA. Their Key Products are Windows OS, Office Suite, Azure (cloud services), and Xbox. Microsoft is a multinational technology company known for its software products and services.

ii. **Apple** was founded in 1976, and its headquarters is in Cupertino, California. Their essential products are iPhone, iPad, Mac, Apple Watch, iOS, and macOS. Apple is a leading technology company specializing in consumer electronics, software, and services.

iii. **Amazon:** was founded in 1994 and its headquarters is in Seattle, Washington, USA. Their essential products are e-commerce, cloud computing (Amazon Web Services), and Kindle. Amazon is the world's largest online retailer and a major player in cloud computing.

iv. **Tesla:** was founded in 2003 and their headquarters is in Palo Alto, California: Its essential products are electric vehicles, solar energy products, and energy storage solutions. Tesla is known for its innovative electric vehicles and sustainable energy solutions.

v. **IBM** was founded in 1911 and their headquarters is in Armonk, New York, USA: Their essential products are enterprise software, hardware, cloud computing, and artificial intelligence. IBM is a multinational technology and consulting company focusing on enterprise solutions.

vi. **Alphabet** was founded in 2015 and its headquarters is in Mountain View, California, USA. Their essential products are Google, YouTube, Android, and Waymo. Alphabet is the parent company of Google and several other businesses involved in technology and innovation.

vii. **Facebook:** was founded in 2004 and its headquarters is in Menlo Park, California, USA. Their essential products are Facebook, Instagram, WhatsApp, and Oculus. Facebook is a social media giant and a major player in the tech industry.

viii. **SpaceX** was founded in 2002 and its headquarters is in Hawthorne, California. Their essential products are space exploration, satellite launches, and reusable rockets. SpaceX, or Space Exploration Technologies Corp., is a private aerospace manufacturer and space transportation company.

ix. **Airbnb** was founded in 2008 and their headquarters is in San Francisco, California. Their Key Product is an Online marketplace for lodging and travel experiences. Airbnb is a platform that connects travelers with hosts offering unique accommodations.

x. **The Walt Disney Company** was founded in 1923 and its headquarters is in Burbank, California. Their essential products are entertainment, media, and theme parks. Disney is a diversified multinational mass media and entertainment conglomerate.

xi. **Sony** was founded in 1946 and their headquarters is in Tokyo, Japan. Their essential products are electronics, gaming, and entertainment. Sony is a global conglomerate focusing on electronics, gaming, and entertainment.

xii. **Pfizer** was founded in 1849 and their headquarters is in New York City, New York, USA. Their essential products are pharmaceuticals, vaccines, and consumer healthcare. Pfizer is a major pharmaceutical company focusing on researching, developing, and manufacturing healthcare products.

xiii. **Samsung:** was founded in 1938 and its headquarters is in Seoul, South Korea. Their essential products are electronics, smartphones, and appliances. Samsung is a multinational conglomerate with many businesses, including electronics and technology.

xiv. **Twiga Foods** was founded in 2014, and its headquarters is in Nairobi, Kenya. Their Key Product is a B2B e-commerce platform for fresh produce. Twiga Foods is a Kenyan company that operates a technology-driven platform connecting farmers to urban retailers to supply fresh produce.

xv. **Apollo Agriculture** was founded in 2016, and its headquarters is in Nairobi, Kenya. Their Key Product is a Digital farming platform for smallholder farmers. Apollo Agriculture leverages data and technology to provide smallholder farmers in Africa with access to financing, high-quality farm inputs, and customized advice.

xvi. **Buu Pass** was founded in 2015 and its headquarters is in Nairobi, Kenya. Their Key Product is a Digital bus ticketing platform. Buu Pass is a Kenyan startup that provides a digital platform for bus ticketing, making it easier for passengers to book and pay for bus rides.

Dynamics of the Strategy

The push strategy involves creating new market spaces by seeking untapped opportunities where competition is scarce or nonexistent. Businesses that follow this strategy thrive by offering unique value propositions and making a leap in value for customers and themselves. They challenge the conventional boundaries of industries, redefine their scope, and explore opportunities beyond traditional market expectations. While technological advancements are not excluded, they push businesses to extend beyond technological innovation. They are encouraged to innovate, including business models, processes, and customer value delivery.

Push businesses shift the focus from competition to collaboration, aligning their activities with customer needs rather than engaging in cutthroat competition with rivals. They consider existing customers and noncustomers outside the current market. By identifying and addressing the needs of noncustomers, companies seek to tap into new demand.

Sustainable growth through continuous innovation is the key to pushing businesses' success. They focus on staying ahead of the curve by consistently innovating and adapting to changing market dynamics. Tesla's entry into the electric car market is an excellent example of the push strategy, combining sustainability with cutting-edge technology and creating a push market. Their focus on innovation and environmental consciousness has sustained their growth.

Random Quotes

❖ You need some terrible things in your life to blossom.

❖ If it is not you, then who?...

2.3 CHAPTER THREE

PULL & PUSH STRATEGY

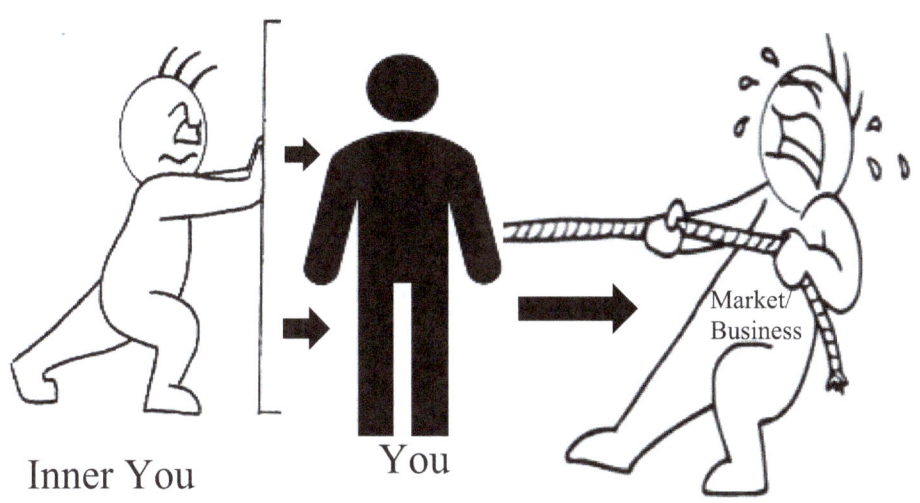

Inner You   You

E ntrepreneurship has given rise to two distinct strategies: the Push and Pull Strategy. Each method has unique features, advantages, and considerations that cater to entrepreneurs' diverse aspirations and approaches. In this chapter, we will delve into the intricacies of both strategies and explore how entrepreneurs can strategically utilize them to achieve success.

The Push Strategy

The Push Strategy embodies the purest form of entrepreneurial spirit. It is driven by an internal force that compels individuals to pursue specific business domains. This strategy is not based on identified market gaps or perceived opportunities; it comes from a deep-seated passion that must be addressed.

Critical Characteristics of Push Strategy

1. **Internal Push:** Push Strategy businesses are characterized by an internal drive that compels entrepreneurs to start and pursue a specific business idea. This intrinsic motivation sets them apart from other ventures.

2. **Autonomy in Training:** Unlike specific business models that necessitate specialized training, Push Strategy businesses often align with the natural skills and inclinations of the entrepreneur. This autonomy in training allows individuals to rely on their inherent abilities—God-given capabilities/gifts/talents.

3. **Innovation and Novelty**: Push Strategy businesses are frequently associated with innovation and novelty. Entrepreneurs adopting this strategy often delve into uncharted territories, introducing new inventions or groundbreaking concepts to the market.

4. **Early-Stage Advantage**: The early stages of a Push Strategy business are characterized by a lack of direct competition. The novelty and uniqueness of these ventures during their inception

create a favorable environment for entrepreneurs to establish a foothold with less immediate competition.

5. **Reduced Regulatory Constraints:** Push Strategy businesses often face reduced regulatory constraints in the nascent stages. The absence of established precedents or well-defined norms allows for greater freedom in operations.

6. **Proactive Client Engagement:** Entrepreneurs employing the Push Strategy must actively seek out clients, customers, or consumers. This proactive engagement requires a deep understanding of the target audience to customize products or services to meet specific needs.

7. **Customization for Client Satisfaction**: The success of Push Strategy businesses hinges on the customization of products or services to align with the needs and wants of the target audience. This personalized approach establishes a direct connection with clientele, fostering loyalty.

Challenges and Considerations

While the Push Strategy offers autonomy and a unique entrepreneurial drive, it comes with challenges. Continuous innovation is imperative to stay ahead, and entrepreneurs must navigate evolving market dynamics and emerging trends.

Pull Strategy: Attracting Success

In contrast to the internal impetus of the Push Strategy, the Pull Strategy is characterized by external factors that attract entrepreneurs into specific business ventures. This approach hinges on identified market gaps, demand in the market, or the charm of profit and prestige. Pull Strategy businesses entice individuals to enter the entrepreneurial arena based on external factors.

Critical Characteristics of Pull Strategy

1. **Market Attraction:** Pull Strategy businesses are initiated based on identified market gaps, demand, or external factors that attract entrepreneurs. The entrepreneur is drawn into the business by external opportunities rather than an internal drive.

2. **Market Research and Demand**: Entrepreneurs adopting the Pull Strategy conduct thorough market research to understand existing and potential market demand. The focus is on anticipating trends and aligning offerings with evolving customer needs.

3. **Brand Prestige**: Pull Strategy businesses often leverage brand prestige or recognition. Entrepreneurs invest in creating a solid brand identity that communicates trust, quality, and reliability, attracting customers through the brand's allure.

4. **Community Engagement**: Businesses employing the Pull Strategy actively engage with the community. By participating in local events and supporting community initiatives, these ventures contribute positively to society, enhancing brand reputation.

5. **Ease of Market Entry**: Pull Strategy businesses are relatively easy to start. The ease of entry is attributed to the business model being well-established and familiar, with entrepreneurs replicating proven approaches.

6. **Competitive Environment**: Due to the ease of entry, Pull Strategy businesses often face stiff competition. Entrepreneurs must establish a competitive advantage through superior customer service, innovative features, or unique value propositions.

7. **Market Changes Monitoring**: A crucial aspect of the Pull Strategy is monitoring market changes. Entrepreneurs must regularly assess customer preferences, competitor activities, and external factors to adapt strategies and stay relevant.

8. **Due Diligence**: Thorough due diligence is emphasized before starting a Pull Strategy business. Entrepreneurs must ensure their business meets the hallmarks of a good company, solving specific problems, being sustainable, and having a straightforward target customer.

Challenges and Considerations

Businesses that adopt a Pull Strategy and seek external opportunities to attract entrepreneurs often encounter specific challenges. In a highly competitive environment, it is crucial to maintain a constant focus on innovation and differentiation. Entrepreneurs must also exercise caution and conduct thorough due diligence before entering the market while remaining adaptable to changes in the market.

Strategic Fusion: Harmonizing Push and Pull

Combining Push and Pull Strategies can be a winning approach for entrepreneurs. By leveraging the internal drive and innovation of the Push Strategy and taking advantage of the Pull Strategy's external opportunities and market demand, entrepreneurs can create a comprehensive and adaptable strategy. This enables them to navigate challenges and seize opportunities for success effectively.

Key Elements of Strategic Fusion

1. **Innovative Agility**: Combine the innovation inherent in Push Strategy with the agility to respond to external market demands. This allows entrepreneurs to introduce novel concepts while remaining responsive to evolving customer needs.

2. **Brand Development**: Infuse the brand development principles of Pull Strategy into Push Strategy businesses. Building a solid brand identity enhances customer trust and loyalty, creating a positive feedback loop.

3. **Proactive Market Research**: Adopt a proactive approach to market research, incorporating the thorough analysis characteristic of the Pull Strategy into the strategic planning of the Push Strategy.

Anticipate trends and align innovations with evolving market demands.

4. **Continuous Learning**: While Push Strategy relies on internal skills, entrepreneurs should continuously learn to stay abreast of industry trends and advancements. This proactive approach ensures sustained relevance and competitiveness.

5. **Community-Centric Approach**: Blend the community engagement aspect of the Pull Strategy with the customization focus of the Push Strategy. This community-centric approach fosters a positive brand image while tailoring products or services to meet local needs.

Strategic Fusion in Action

Imagine an entrepreneur who has developed a unique technological innovation driven by their internal motivation. To ensure success, they need to combine Push and Pull strategies. This means conducting market research to identify external demand and adapting their innovation to meet specific customer needs. They must also develop a brand that conveys trust and reliability, engages with the community, and presents positive contributions. By using a synergistic approach that combines internal drive with external market alignment, the entrepreneur can position their business for success.

Entrepreneurs have two distinct avenues for success: the Push and Pull Strategies. By strategically combining these approaches, entrepreneurs can create a holistic and adaptable business strategy that will help them navigate challenges, leverage opportunities, and achieve sustained success in the dynamic landscape of entrepreneurship. Understanding the nuances of both approaches is critical to successfully implementing them.

How to use the Pull and push Strategy to your advantage

Entrepreneurs, at the helm of their ventures, are faced with the strategic choice between two distinctive yet complementary approaches—Push Strategy and Pull Strategy. Navigating the entrepreneurial landscape requires a nuanced understanding of how these strategies can be synergistically employed to maximize advantages and overcome challenges.

The synergy between Push and Pull Strategy lies in the strategic integration of their essential elements. Entrepreneurs can leverage the internal drive and innovation intrinsic to the Push Strategy while simultaneously capitalizing on the external market opportunities and demand identification characteristic of the Pull Strategy. This amalgamation fosters a holistic and adaptive entrepreneurial approach.

1. Innovative Agility

Push Strategy: The internal Push-driving Push Strategy often leads to innovative and groundbreaking ideas. Entrepreneurs can harness this creative agility to introduce novel concepts and technological advancements.

Pull Strategy: By proactively conducting market research and identifying external demand, entrepreneurs can align their innovations with market needs. This ensures a thorough understanding of customer preferences and industry trends, which complements the internal drive for innovation.

2. Brand Development

Push Strategy: The autonomy in training and inherent skills associated with Push Strategy can be leveraged for personal branding. Entrepreneurs can build a solid personal brand, emphasizing their expertise and commitment to innovation.

Pull Strategy: Infusing the brand development principles of Pull Strategy, entrepreneurs can create a brand identity that communicates trust, reliability, and customer-centric values. This enhances the market perception of the business, attracting customers through the allure of a reputable brand.

3. Proactive Market Research

Push Strategy: While internal motivations drive Push Strategy, entrepreneurs can proactively engage in market research to anticipate trends and align innovations with emerging market demands. This ensures that the inner drive is complemented by external market alignment.

Pull Strategy: The thorough market research characteristic of the Pull Strategy can be integrated into the strategic planning of the Push Strategy. Entrepreneurs can identify market gaps, assess competition, and tailor their offerings to meet customer needs.

4. Continuous Learning

Push Strategy: Entrepreneurs relying on inherent skills can embrace continuous learning to stay abreast of industry trends and advancements. This proactive approach ensures that internal skills are continuously honed and adapted to evolving market dynamics.

Pull Strategy: The adaptability and responsiveness to market changes inherent in the Pull Strategy can be adopted by entrepreneurs following the Push approach. This involves a commitment to continuous learning and a willingness to adjust strategies based on external market shifts.

5. Community-Centric Approach:

Push Strategy: Entrepreneurs can infuse the customization focus of Push Strategy with a community-centric approach. By understanding the target audience's needs, entrepreneurs can tailor products or services to meet local demands, creating a personalized connection with customers.

Pull Strategy: The community engagement aspect of Pull Strategy can be integrated into Push Strategy businesses. Actively participating in local events, supporting community initiatives, and displaying positive contributions enhance the brand image and foster a sense of community involvement.

Overcoming Challenges

1. **Continuous Learning Culture**:   The fusion of Push and Pull requires a commitment to a continuous learning culture. Entrepreneurs must stay informed about industry trends, customer preferences, and emerging technologies to navigate challenges and adapt to market changes.

2. **Agile Market Strategies:**   An integrated approach necessitates agile market strategies. Entrepreneurs must be ready to adjust their business models, products, or services based on internal innovations and external market shifts, ensuring resilience in the face of challenges.

3. **Balancing Autonomy and External Alignment:**   Striking the right balance between internal autonomy and external market alignment is crucial. Entrepreneurs must ensure that their internal drive for innovation aligns with identified market opportunities, avoiding potential disconnects that could hinder success.

Examples of businesses that use pull and push strategy

As push and pull might seem complicated, several companies have successfully used the strategy. The following are some of the e.gs;

1. Safaricom PLC:

12: credit to Safaricom PLC

Safaricom is a telecommunications company based in Kenya, and it's one of Africa's leading mobile network operators. Established in 1997, Safaricom has played a pivotal role in transforming communication in Kenya and the East African region. The company provides various telecommunications services, including mobile money transfer (M Pesa), voice, data, and financial services.

Key Success Factors

1. M Pesa Innovation: Safaricom revolutionized mobile payments through its M Pesa service, enabling millions of people to transfer money, pay bills, and access financial services easily.

2. Market Dominance: Safaricom has maintained a dominant position in the Kenyan telecommunications market, boasting a large and loyal customer base.

3. Network Infrastructure: The company has invested significantly in building a robust and extensive network infrastructure, ensuring reliable connectivity across urban and rural areas.

4. Customer-Centric Approach: Safaricom's focus on customer satisfaction and user-friendly services has contributed to its strong brand reputation and customer loyalty.

2. Raiply:

13: Credit to Kenya Business Directory

Raiply is a leading forestry and timber processing company in East Africa. Founded in 1986, the company is known for sustainable forestry practices and for producing high-quality wood and timber products. Raiply operates in Kenya and Tanzania, contributing to the region's economic development through responsible forestry and manufacturing.

Key Success Factors:

1. Sustainable Forestry Practices: Raiply's commitment to sustainable forestry management ensures the long-term availability of timber resources while minimizing environmental impact.

2. Quality Products: The company focuses on producing top-quality wood and timber products, meeting local and international standards, which has helped it establish a strong market presence.

3. Community Engagement: Raiply engages with local communities, creating a positive social impact through employment opportunities, community development projects, and environmental conservation initiatives.

4. Diversification: Raiply has adapted to changing market demands by diversifying its product range, ensuring a stable and resilient business model.

Dynamics of the Strategy

The Push and Pull Strategy dynamics in entrepreneurship are intricately woven into innovation, market responsiveness, and strategic adaptation. Understanding the dynamics of these two approaches is essential for entrepreneurs seeking to navigate the complexities of the business landscape. Let's delve into the dynamics of the Push and Pull Strategy, drawing insights from the detailed discussions above.

Dynamics of Push Strategy

1. Internal Drive and Innovation: Dynamic Force: Push Strategy is characterized by an internal Push, an innate force that drives entrepreneurs to innovate. This inner drive is a dynamic force propelling individuals to explore new ideas, concepts, and technological advancements.

Inherent Skills: Entrepreneurs relying on Push Strategy often find themselves equipped with inherent skills. These technical, creative, or managerial skills form the foundation for innovative endeavors driven by internal motivation.

2. **Autonomy and Agility**: Autonomous Decision Making: Push Strategy gives entrepreneurs a high degree of autonomy in decision making. The freedom to pursue innovative ideas without external constraints fosters agility and adaptability.

Agile Innovation: The dynamic nature of the Push Strategy allows for agile innovation. Entrepreneurs can swiftly adapt to emerging trends, refine their ideas based on feedback, and iterate their products or services to meet evolving market demands.

3. **Personal Brand Development:** Entrepreneurial Identity: Push Strategy encourages entrepreneurs to develop strong identities. The emphasis is on personal brand development, showcasing the entrepreneur's expertise, vision, and commitment to innovation. Differentiation: The dynamic of personal brand development in Push Strategy is a differentiation factor. Entrepreneurs discover a unique identity, positioning themselves as innovative leaders in their respective industries.

4. **Continuous Learning Culture:** Proactive Learning: Entrepreneurs following the Push Strategy cultivate a continuous learning culture. The dynamic of continuous learning involves staying abreast of industry trends and technological advancements and acquiring new skills to fuel ongoing innovation.

Dynamics of Pull Strategy

1. **External Market Alignment:** Identified Market Opportunities: Pull Strategy revolves around identified market opportunities and external factors that attract entrepreneurs. The dynamic lies in entrepreneurs actively seeking market gaps, demand signals, and opportunities aligning with their business goals.

Proactive Market Research: The dynamic nature of the Pull Strategy involves proactive market research. Entrepreneurs dynamically engage with the market, conducting thorough analyses to understand customer needs, industry trends, and potential areas for business growth.

2. **Brand Prestige and Community Engagement:** Building Brand Prestige: Pull Strategy often involves building prestige. The dynamic of brand building focuses on creating a favorable market perception, emphasizing trust, quality, and reliability to attract customers.

Community-Centric Approach: Pull Strategy dynamically engages with the community. Entrepreneurs actively participate in community events, support local initiatives, and showcase positive contributions, fostering a community-centric approach that enhances brand reputation.

3. **Ease of Market Entry and Competitive Environment:**

Low Entry Barriers: Pull Strategy is characterized by its relative ease of market entry. The dynamic of low entry barriers allows entrepreneurs to initiate businesses based on established models or proven concepts.

Stiff Competition: The ease of entry, however, leads to a dynamic of stiff competition. Pull Strategy businesses often face intense competition, necessitating entrepreneurs to establish competitive advantages to thrive in the market.

4. **Market Changes Monitoring and Due Diligence**

Adapting to Market Changes: The pull Strategy requires entrepreneurs to adapt to market changes dynamically. The dynamic nature of monitoring market shifts allows entrepreneurs to adjust strategies, refine products or services, and remain responsive to evolving customer preferences.

Thorough Due Diligence: Entrepreneurs employing Pull Strategy dynamically conduct thorough due diligence. The dynamic of due diligence involves ensuring that the business meets the hallmarks of a good company, solves specific problems, is sustainable, and has a straightforward target customer.

Synergistic Dynamics: Leveraging the Push Pull Fusion

1. **Innovative Agility and Market Differentiation:** The push and pull strategy of constructive collaboration enables entrepreneurs to achieve innovative agility and market differentiation. The internal drive for innovation (Push) aligns with identified market opportunities (Pull), creating a dynamic blend that sets the business apart while continuously adapting to market dynamics.

2. **Brand Development and Adaptive Innovation:** Combining Push's personal brand development with Pull's community engagement fosters a dynamic brand image. This emotional brand development is a foundation for adaptive innovation, allowing entrepreneurs to stay relevant and resonate with evolving customer expectations.

3. **Continuous Learning Culture and Agile Market Strategies:** The push and pull strategy fusion cultivates a continuous learning culture. Entrepreneurs dynamically engage in ongoing learning to fuel internal innovation and external market responsiveness. This dynamic learning culture translates into agile market strategies that adjust to changing conditions.

4. **Balancing Autonomy and External Alignment:** Striking the right balance between internal autonomy and external market alignment is a dynamic challenge. Entrepreneurs must dynamically

navigate the interplay between internal drive and external opportunities, ensuring a harmonious fusion that drives business success.

Random Quotes

- ❖ You have no say in what happens to you, but you have a say in what you do about it.
- ❖ Life is 10% what happens to you and 90% what you do about it.

3.0 PART 3: CONCLUSION

3.1 CHAPTER ONE

SUMMARY

Many businesses fail due to the unrealistic expectations of their entrepreneurs. They believe that their products or services will immediately gain huge demand and generate profits after launch. However, this belief is often far from reality, resulting in the entrepreneur feeling like a failure and ultimately leading to the closure of the business. Eric Ries' book, "The Lean Startup," uses this analogy to explain the importance of testing and iterating your product or service before launching to ensure its success.

Learning what your customers want and understanding the type of business you want to start before launching a successful business/product is essential. The interplay of pull, push, and Push and Pull Strategy offers entrepreneurs a comprehensive and adaptable framework for success in the search for the right entrepreneurial strategies.

The Push Strategy showcases the power of internal drive, innovation, and autonomous decision-making. Entrepreneurs driven by an internal push find themselves equipped with inherent skills that foster a continuous learning culture, propelling agile innovation. Personal brand development becomes a hallmark, differentiating entrepreneurs and positioning them as innovative leaders in their respective fields.

On the other hand, the Pull Strategy unveils the art of external market alignment, brand prestige, and community engagement. Entrepreneurs employing the Pull Strategy should seek out identified market opportunities and conduct proactive market research to understand customer needs and industry trends. Building a prestigious brand should be paramount, and having a community-centric approach will foster a positive contribution, enhancing the overall brand image. However, the ease of market entry in the Pull Strategy introduces stiff competition, urging entrepreneurs to establish competitive advantages.

The strategic fusion of the Push and Pull Strategy should become the number one strategy for every entrepreneur, especially those unsure if they should choose the pull or push strategy. Entrepreneurs can capitalize on the internal drive for innovation while capitalizing on external market opportunities, creating a harmonious blend that sets their ventures apart. The fusion allows for innovative agility, brand development, and continuous learning, creating a great constructive collaboration that propels businesses toward sustained success. Striking a balance between autonomy and external alignment becomes challenging, requiring entrepreneurs to navigate the interplay between internal motivations and external opportunities.

When starting a business, choosing between pull, push, and the Push and Pull Strategy demands a great understanding of a person's external and internal environment. Entrepreneurs should choose the environment that offers the best chances of business success. The dynamics of inner drive, autonomous decision-making, market alignment, and community engagement provide a rich tapestry for entrepreneurs to weave their success stories.

The strategic fusion of the Push and Pull Strategy emerges as a powerful choreography. It allows entrepreneurs to navigate challenges, leverage opportunities, and chart a course toward sustained success in the ever-evolving entrepreneurial landscape. As entrepreneurs embrace the dynamics of both strategies, they position themselves as innovators and adaptive leaders ready to thrive in the dynamic business world.

STEP 1
- Choose the a Strategy (Push or Pull)
- Identify the problem you would like to solve
- come up with the vision, mision and co-values
- Write down all the resources and skills needed

STEP 2
- Do market research
- Choose a business name
- Choose your business location
- Draft a business plan

STEP 3
- Develop/ source/ create your product/ service
- Develop your marketing and market entry plan
- Check the entrepreneurs check list
- Launch your business

STEP 4
- Offer the best customer service experience
- Listen to your customers

STEP 5
- Keep good record of all the transactions in the business
- Maintain/ manage your cost

STEP 6
- continously learn and improve
- Costantly Check the health of your business and do market reseach
- Remain focus on the vision and vision

Random Quotes

❖ Life is going to whoop you until you surrender if you don't do what you have to do, even if you don't like it.

❖ Life is not about how long you live; it's all about what you leave behind when you leave

3.2 CHAPTER TWO

PERSONAL NOTES

This section of my notes is crucial, and I am confident it will provide valuable insights. Even if you missed some information in the previous chapters, don't worry I've got you covered. I'll highlight the most essential points to make things easier for you. I aim to ensure you gain a deeper understanding of the subject matter and find value in this segment. So, let's dive in with confidence!

Pitfalls in Entrepreneurship

14: Credit To: https://www.marketcircle.com

1. Lack of Clear Vision and Planning:

Pitfall: The primary mistake entrepreneurs make is jumping into business without a clear vision and strategic plan. This can lead to a lack of direction and make it challenging to achieve long-term success.

Solution: Before launching a business, take the time to define your vision, mission, and objectives. Develop a comprehensive business plan that outlines your goals, target market, competition, and financial projections. A well-thought-out plan serves as a roadmap for your entrepreneurial journey.

2. **Ignoring Market Research:**

Pitfall: Failure to conduct thorough market research can result in a misalignment between your product or service and the actual needs of your target market. This oversight can lead to poor product market fit and hinder growth.

Solution: Invest time and resources in market research to understand your target audience, industry trends, and competitors. Identify gaps in the market and validate the demand for your product or service before launching. Regularly update your market research to stay informed about evolving customer preferences.

3. **Underestimating Financial Management:**

Pitfall: Inadequate financial planning and management are common pitfalls that can lead to cash flow problems, debt accumulation, and business failure.

Solution: Develop a detailed financial plan that includes startup costs, operating expenses, revenue projections, and a realistic timeline for profitability. Monitor your finances regularly, control expenses, and establish an emergency fund for unexpected challenges. Consider seeking the advice of financial experts or mentors to ensure sound financial management.

4. Ignoring the Importance of Marketing:

Pitfall: Neglecting marketing efforts can result in a lack of visibility and customer acquisition. Even the best products or services need effective marketing to reach their target audience.

Solution: Develop a robust marketing strategy that includes online and offline channels. Utilize social media, content marketing, and search engine optimization to increase brand awareness. Regularly evaluate and adjust your marketing tactics based on performance metrics and customer feedback.

5. Poor Team Dynamics and Leadership:

Pitfall: Building a successful business requires effective leadership and a cohesive team. Ignoring the importance of team dynamics can lead to communication breakdowns, low morale, and decreased productivity.

Solution: Invest time in building a strong, motivated team. Communicate your vision, values, and expectations. Foster open communication and encourage collaboration. Lead by example and address conflicts promptly. Regularly assess and enhance your team's skills through training and professional development.

6. Scaling Too Quickly or Slowly:

Pitfall: Incorrectly timing the scaling of your business can be detrimental. Scaling too quickly without proper infrastructure can lead to operational chaos, while climbing too slowly may result in missed opportunities.

Solution: Monitor key performance indicators (KPIs) closely and scale your business in a controlled manner. Assess your capacity for growth, invest in scalable systems, and ensure your team can handle increased demand. Regularly review your business plan to align scaling strategies with market conditions.

7. **Overlooking Legal and Regulatory Compliance**:

Pitfall: Ignoring legal and regulatory requirements can lead to fines, lawsuits, and damage to your business's reputation. Compliance issues can arise in licensing, intellectual property, and employment practices.

Solution: Consult legal professionals to ensure your business complies with all relevant laws and regulations. Stay informed about industry-specific requirements and changes in legislation. Implement proper contracts, agreements, and intellectual property protection measures to safeguard your business interests.

8. **Ignoring Customer Feedback:**

Pitfall: Disregarding customer feedback can result in a product or service not meeting customer expectations. This oversight can lead to a decline in customer satisfaction and loyalty.

Solution: Actively seek and listen to customer feedback through surveys, reviews, and direct communication. Use customer input to improve your products, services, and customer experience continuously. Establish a customer-centric culture within your organization to build solid and lasting relationships.

9. **Inadequate Risk Management**:

Pitfall: Every business faces risks, from market fluctuations to unforeseen events like natural disasters. Failing to identify and manage these risks can lead to significant setbacks.

Solution: Conduct a comprehensive risk assessment to identify potential threats to your business. Develop a risk management plan, including strategies for mitigating, transferring, or accepting risks. Regularly reassess and update your risk management plan as your business evolves.

10. **Lack of Adaptability and Innovation**:

Pitfall: Markets are dynamic, and businesses must adapt to changing conditions. Failing to innovate and evolve can result in obsolescence and loss of competitiveness.

Solution: Foster a culture of innovation within your organization. Stay abreast of industry trends, invest in research and development, and encourage employees to contribute ideas. Be open to change and ready to pivot your business model if necessary.

Navigating the entrepreneurial landscape requires strategic planning, adaptability, and continuous learning. By avoiding these common pitfalls, aspiring entrepreneurs can increase their chances of building a successful and sustainable business. Proactively addressing challenges also helps. Seek mentorship, stay informed about industry trends, and learn from successes and failures. Entrepreneurship is a dynamic process. The ability to learn and adapt is as important as the initial vision that sparks the entrepreneurial spirit.

Key Takeaways

Now, to emphasize some points. I will expound on and break the above segment into three main parts. The first is before you start the business. The second is after you have created it. The third is when you wish to close or end the business.

1. Before you start any business:

- Do proper research (market research). In most cases, if possible, seek professional help to guide you on doing excellent or actual market research.
- Don`t start a business because your friend or enemy has started; and somehow, they seem to be doing well, to be like them.
- Have a business plan that is not primarily motivated by the excellent return on investment but by the value the business will add to the lives of the targeted customers. Your business plan should focus on how big or good the solution you provide is rather than how big or profitable the business is/will be.

- Have a basic understanding of how the industry you want to invest in works before you invest. For instance, starting a matatu business is madness if you don't understand how the transport industry works.
- Don't start purely to make money; sometimes, most businesses are not profitable for years.
- Don't start to prove someone wrong. Otherwise, the business will prove you wrong.
- Try to find a problem you can solve and get to know who the issue is explicitly affecting, then create a business around it.
- Have realistic expectations; you are starting a business, not a magic workshop where only good things happen magically within a short period without much work.
- Don't invest 100% of your resources; invest a maximum of 80% of your resources.
- Get someone who can guide you; entrepreneurship should not be lonely. Have a mentor, a coach, or a teacher
- Get your vision right, and ensure it's so good or potent; the stronger it is, the easier the process will be.
- Don't start to take care of your immediate personal needs; remember that human needs are insatiable and endless. (Your needs will finish your business). Start to take care of other people's problems, for the more problems you solve, the more money you make.

- Don't start so that you can work for fewer hours, work less hard, and make more money. Starting a business will make you work longer hours, work harder, and probably make less money.
- Be ready to be very disciplined, patient, and humble. Otherwise, you will be closing the business within the first six months.
- Be ready to be corrected/guided by anyone, i.e., your employees, clients, strangers, etc. Sometimes, the guidance can be indirect, and it is worth noting that indirect guidance can come from any source or anyone, including your competitors and your enemies. Be wise to take the right guidance/correction and ignore the wrong ones.

2. After you have started any business (when you are managing or running any business:

- If you don't remain focused on the vision of the business, you lose your business.
- Constantly learn new trends in your respective industry; things are not static, and thus you should not.
- Get someone who can hold you accountable for all your actions in your business; it's not enough to keep yourself accountable.
- Monitor all your expenses and find ways to reduce or maintain them. The lower your costs, the higher your profits.

- Separate your finances from the business finances. It would be best if you only used the salary from the business to take care of personal issues.
- Have proper records of all the transactions happening in your business.
- Understand your client's needs and discover how the service or goods you sell can better and more sustainably solve their needs.
- Be flexible
- Think of ways you can sell your services or offer your services in a better way
- Customers are the kings and queens; thus, treat each of them as one.
- Constantly train yourself and your employees in all the aspects of your business.
- Constantly let your clients know your unique selling proposition.
- Don't take liabilities (loans) you have not planned for.

3. When you want to end/ close your business:
- Confirm if the vision has been achieved; if not, get someone else to continue the business. If you don't have any vision, just end the business. (But read the following points as well)

- Evaluate the cost of the business; this will be helpful if you wish to sell the business or when you want to settle the debts that the company may have accrued throughout its days of operations.
- Think about the possibilities of a buyout or merger.
- Have a clear plan on the way forward without the business in your life.
- Know that it's not the end but the beginning of a new thing, a new thing that finds you better than the way you were when you were starting.
- Note down all the things you have been doing or have done right and wrong; this will help you avoid the mistakes next time and also help you know what to do in the next business you might intend to start.
- Get an expert to try and help you get your business on track, that is, if your reason for closing was due to a bad-performing business.

The final point to have at the back of your mind is that starting a business during a recession or economic downturn is too risky and may not be profitable.

Myths and Misconceptions in Entrepreneurship

Entrepreneurship is a challenging journey often misunderstood due to common myths and misconceptions. This section aims to dispel such myths and offer insights through e.gs, illuminating the realities of the entrepreneurial landscape

1. Myth: Entrepreneurship Guarantees Overnight Success

Reality: Entrepreneurial success is a gradual process that requires dedication, resilience, and often, years of hard work. The notion of overnight success is a pervasive myth. Take the example of Jeff Bezos, who founded Amazon in 1994. The company experienced years of losses before becoming the e-commerce giant we know today.

2. Myth: Entrepreneurs Are Born, Not Made

Reality: While certain personality traits may predispose individuals to entrepreneurship, anyone can cultivate the necessary skills and mindset. Successful entrepreneurs come from diverse backgrounds. Oprah Winfrey, for instance, emerged from a challenging childhood to build a media empire through determination and adaptability.

3. Myth: Entrepreneurs Must Take Huge Risks to Succeed

Reality: Strategic risk-taking is essential, but it doesn't always equate to betting on the farm. Sensible risk management is a hallmark of successful entrepreneurs. Elon Musk, founder of

SpaceX and Tesla, is known for calculated risks, carefully weighing potential rewards against potential losses.

4. Myth: Entrepreneurs Only Need a Great Idea

Reality: Execution is as crucial as the idea itself. Countless great ideas falter without effective implementation. Consider the case of Xerox PARC, which developed ground-breaking technologies but struggled to commercialize them. Apple's Steve Jobs recognized the potential and successfully implemented these innovations.

5. Myth: Success Comes from Doing It Alone

Reality: Collaborations and partnerships are often instrumental in entrepreneurial success. Bill Gates and Paul Allen co-founded Microsoft, and their partnership played a pivotal role in the company's growth. Networking and building a strong support system contribute significantly to success.

6. Myth: All Entrepreneurs Must Be Young and Tech-Savvy

Reality: Entrepreneurship knows no age limits. Numerous successful entrepreneurs, such as Ray Kroc (McDonald's) and Colonel Harland Sanders (KFC), achieved monumental success later in life. Experience and wisdom can be valuable assets in entrepreneurship.

7. Myth: Entrepreneurs Only Work on Passion Projects

Reality: While passion is vital, successful entrepreneurs often engage in projects that align with market demand. Mark Zuckerberg, for instance, pivoted Facebook from a college social platform to a global network based on user needs and market trends.

8. Myth: A College Degree is Necessary for Entrepreneurial Success

Reality: Many successful entrepreneurs, including Bill Gates (Microsoft), Steve Jobs (Apple), and Mark Zuckerberg (Facebook), dropped out of college to pursue their entrepreneurial endeavors. A formal education can be beneficial, but it's not a prerequisite for success.

9. Myth: Entrepreneurs Enjoy Unlimited Freedom and Flexibility

Reality: While entrepreneurship offers autonomy, it also demands an unparalleled level of dedication and responsibility. Entrepreneurs often work longer hours and face more stress than traditional employees. The freedom comes with the responsibility to steer the ship successfully.

10. Myth: Failure Means the End of the Road

Reality: Failure is a natural part of entrepreneurship, and many successful entrepreneurs have faced setbacks. Walt Disney's first animation company went bankrupt before he created the iconic Disney brand. Learning from failure is integral to entrepreneurial growth.

Hiring and Recruiting Right

Hiring the right people is a critical aspect of starting a business. Here are some tips to help you build a strong and effective team:

1. Clearly Define Roles and Responsibilities: Clearly outline the roles and responsibilities for each position before starting the recruitment process. Develop detailed job descriptions that highlight key responsibilities, required skills, and qualifications.

2. Understand Your Company Culture: Identify the values and culture you want to foster within your company. During the recruitment process, assess candidates not only for their skills but also for their alignment with your company's culture.

3. Leverage Online Job Platforms: Utilize online job platforms and websites to reach a broader audience. Platforms like LinkedIn, Indeed, and Glassdoor can help you connect with potential candidates.

4. Tap into Your Network: Leverage your professional network and connections for referrals. Personal recommendations often result in high-quality candidates who align with your business goals.

5. Create an Engaging Careers Page: Develop a compelling careers page on your business website. Highlight your company's mission, values, and the benefits of working with your organization.

6. Utilize Social Media: Leverage social media platforms to showcase your company culture and job openings. Engage with potential candidates through platforms like LinkedIn, Twitter, and Instagram.

7. Implement Employee Referral Programs: Establish an employee referral program to encourage current employees to refer qualified candidates. Offer incentives or rewards for successful referrals that result in a hire.

8. Conduct Structured Interviews: Develop a set of standardized interview questions for each position. Conduct structured interviews to ensure consistency and fair evaluation of candidates.

9. Assess Soft Skills: Besides technical skills, evaluate candidates for soft skills such as communication, teamwork, and adaptability. Soft skills are crucial for a harmonious and productive work environment.

10. Consider Internship Programs: Implement internship programs to assess potential long-term hires. Internships allow candidates to showcase their skills while giving you the opportunity to evaluate their fit within the company.

11. Provide Growth Opportunities: Highlight growth opportunities within your company during the recruitment process.

   - Emphasize potential career paths and professional development opportunities.

12. Be Transparent About Compensation: Clearly communicate the compensation structure, including salary, benefits, and any performance-related bonuses. Transparency helps build trust with potential hires.

13. Use Skill Assessments: Implement skill assessments or tests relevant to the position. This helps ensure that candidates possess the necessary skills for the role.

14. Conduct Background Checks: Prior to making a final hiring decision, conduct thorough background checks. Verify employment history, educational qualifications, and check references.

15. Prioritize Diversity and Inclusion: Foster a diverse and inclusive workplace by actively seeking candidates from different backgrounds. Diversity enhances creativity and brings varied perspectives to your team.

16. Offer Competitive Benefits: Provide competitive benefits packages to attract top talent. Health insurance, retirement plans, and other perks can make your company more appealing.

17. Maintain a Positive Candidate Experience: Ensure a positive and respectful candidate experience throughout the recruitment process. Communicate promptly, provide feedback, and keep candidates informed.

18. Evaluate Cultural Fit: Assess candidates for their alignment with your company's values and mission. A strong cultural fit contributes to a cohesive and motivated team.

Tactics To Elevate Your Business

Entrepreneurship is a constantly evolving process. I will share tactics that entrepreneurs can use to guide their businesses toward success in an ever-changing marketplace.

1. Cultivate a Growth Mindset: A growth mindset is the cornerstone of entrepreneurial success, fostering resilience, adaptability, and an insatiable appetite for learning.

Action Steps: Infuse your organizational culture with a commitment to continuous learning. Encourage your team to view challenges as opportunities for growth. Embrace failure as a stepping stone to future success.

2. Develop a Robust Business Plan: A meticulously crafted business plan is not just a formality but a dynamic blueprint that guides your business through every phase of its growth.

Action Steps: Clearly articulate your business objectives, mission, and long-term vision. Conduct regular reviews and updates to ensure alignment with market trends. Leverage your business plan as a strategic tool for decision-making.

3. Build a Strong Online Presence: In the digital age, your online presence is your storefront to the world, influencing brand perception, customer engagement, and market reach.

Action Steps: Invest in a visually appealing, user-friendly website that reflects your brand identity. Leverage social media platforms strategically for brand promotion and interaction. Employ effective SEO strategies to enhance your online visibility.

4. Prioritize Customer Experience: A stellar customer experience isn't just a transactional outcome; it's the heart of customer loyalty, positive word-of-mouth, and sustained business growth.

Action Steps: Understand your customers' needs through surveys, feedback, and analytics. Implement responsive customer support channels for swift issue resolution. Go the extra mile to personalize interactions and exceed customer expectations.

5. Embrace Innovation: Innovation is the lifeblood of entrepreneurial success, propelling your business ahead of the curve and ensuring relevance in a rapidly changing market.

Action Steps: Foster a culture that encourages and rewards creative thinking. Invest in research and development to stay ahead of industry trends. Empower your team to contribute innovative ideas and solutions.

6. Strategic Marketing and Branding: Effective marketing and branding are the conduits through which your unique story resonates with your audience, leaving an indelible mark in the market.

Action Steps: Develop a holistic marketing strategy aligned with your target audience and brand identity. Consistently communicate your brand values and narrative across all channels Diversify your marketing efforts, both online and offline, for maximum impact.

7. Financial Management: Prudent financial management is the backbone of business sustainability, requiring meticulous planning, budgeting, and strategic decision-making.

Action Steps: Develop and adhere to a detailed budget, regularly monitoring financial performance. Utilize advanced accounting software for accurate and transparent financial reporting. Explore diverse funding options, managing debt responsibly.

8. Cultivate a High-Performing Team: A motivated, skilled team is the engine that propels your business forward, requiring a positive work culture, professional development, and effective leadership.

Action Steps: Hire individuals who align with your company culture and values. Invest in ongoing training and provide opportunities for skill development. Foster open communication, collaboration, and a sense of shared purpose.

9. Adaptability and Resilience: In an ever-changing business landscape, adaptability and resilience are the armor that shields your business from uncertainties and setbacks.

Action Steps: Stay informed about emerging industry trends and technological advancements. Proactively anticipate and adapt to market changes, remaining agile. Learn from failures, viewing setbacks as invaluable lessons for growth.

10. Networking and Partnerships: Building meaningful professional connections and strategic partnerships opens doors to new opportunities, insights, and collaborative ventures.

Action Steps: Attend industry events, conferences, and networking functions to expand your professional circle. Collaborate with complementary businesses, fostering equally beneficial relationships. Cultivate connections with mentors and industry influencers for guidance and support.

Financial Opportunities for Entrepreneurs

The role of [9]finance in any business is paramount. Finance is not just a means to an end; it is the lifeblood that fuels innovation, sustains growth, and propels businesses toward unprecedented success.

Key Benefits of Finance in Business:

1. Adequate financial resources empower entrepreneurs to expand operations, enter new markets, and invest in innovation.

---

[9] Money is not everything in a business but it is important.

2. Financial planning allows businesses to anticipate and navigate uncertainties, acting as a buffer against unforeseen challenges.

3. Well-managed finances contribute to streamlined operations, optimizing resource allocation, and enhancing overall efficiency.

4. Informed financial insights enable entrepreneurs to make strategic decisions, aligning business objectives with market trends.

5. Sound financial health makes businesses more attractive to potential investors, fostering growth through external funding.

Finance opportunities available for entrepreneurs

1. **Traditional Bank Loans:** Traditional bank loans remain a steadfast option for entrepreneurs seeking capital. With favorable interest rates and structured repayment plans, these loans are suitable for businesses with a solid credit history and stable financials.

2. **Venture Capital**: For startups with high growth potential, venture capital offers an infusion of funds in exchange for equity. This form of financing not only provides capital but often comes with mentorship and strategic guidance from seasoned investors.

3. **Angel Investors**: Angel investors, typically high-net-worth individuals, invest their funds into promising startups. Their involvement goes beyond monetary support, often providing valuable industry expertise and networking opportunities.

4. **Crowdfunding**: The rise of digital platforms has democratized fundraising through crowdfunding. Entrepreneurs can showcase their projects to a wide audience, raising capital from individuals who believe in their vision.

5. **Small Business Grants:** Government agencies, private organizations, and nonprofits offer various grants to support small businesses. These grants, often tailored to specific industries or demographics, provide a financial boost without the burden of repayment.

6. **Bootstrapping:** Entrepreneurs can opt for self-funding or bootstrapping, leveraging personal savings or revenue generated by the business to fuel growth. While it requires financial discipline, bootstrapping allows for complete ownership and control.

7. **Invoice Financing**: For businesses facing cash flow challenges, invoice financing provides a solution. Entrepreneurs can receive immediate cash by selling their outstanding invoices to a third party at a discount.

8. **Peer-to-Peer Lending**: Online platforms facilitate peer-to-peer lending, connecting entrepreneurs with individual lenders. This alternative financing option often offers flexibility in terms and interest rates.

9. **Strategic Partnerships**: Collaborative ventures with strategic partners can inject capital into a business. Entrepreneurs can

explore partnerships where both parties bring unique resources or capabilities to the table.

10. Initial Coin Offerings (ICOs) and Cryptocurrency Funding: In the realm of digital innovation, entrepreneurs can explore ICOs or seek funding through cryptocurrencies. This avenue is gaining popularity, especially within the tech and blockchain sectors.

Symptoms That Call for Urgent Professional Aid

In the intricate dance of business dynamics, the signs and [10]symptoms of a company's health are akin to the signals our bodies send us when something is amiss. Just as early detection is key to personal well-being, recognizing the red flags in a business is vital for its sustained success.

1. **Flatlining Financial Vital Signs:** Imagine a business's financial health as a heartbeat, with cash flow, profit margins, and ROI serving as the life-sustaining pulse. When these vital signs flatline, urgent intervention is warranted.

Symptoms:

- Declining Cash Reserves: - for example A retail chain experiencing dwindling cash reserves due to unforeseen market shifts.

---

[10] A business health should be checked as frequently as you check your own health.

- Consistent Losses: - for example A tech startup facing consecutive quarters of losses due to misjudged product-market fit.
- Inadequate ROI: - for example, an investment portfolio yielding minimal returns despite market opportunities.

Professional Intervention:

A Financial consultant should diagnose the ailment, and prescribe strategies to resuscitate and fortify financial well-being.

2. Employee Burnout: The Silent Pandemic: Much like a person succumbing to chronic fatigue, a business suffering from widespread employee burnout experiences a debilitating decline in productivity.

Symptoms:

- High Turnover Rates: - for example A tech company witnessing top talent leaving due to perpetual burnout.
- Reduced Productivity: - for example, A creative agency grappling with diminished output from fatigued teams.
- Increased Absenteeism: - for example A manufacturing plant facing rising absenteeism due to work-related stress.

Professional Intervention:

Human resources specialists can prescribe remedies, rejuvenating the workforce and restoring a vibrant corporate pulse.

3. Communication Breakdown: The Silent Treatment

Consider communication breakdowns as the corporate equivalent of interpersonal conflicts—a silent treatment that stifles collaboration.

Symptoms:

- Misalignment Between Teams: - for example: A marketing team working in isolation from the sales department, causing misaligned efforts.

- Lack of Transparency: - for example, Leadership withholding crucial information, fostering distrust among employees.

- Frequent Misunderstandings: - for example: Interdepartmental miscommunications leading to project delays and errors.

Professional Intervention:

A Communication expert should prescribe communication therapies, fostering a culture of transparency and collaboration.

4. A Weak Immune System: Vulnerability to External Threats

Just as a compromised immune system makes the body susceptible to illness, a business with a weak risk management system is vulnerable to external threats.

Symptoms:

- Unprepared for Market Changes: - for example A retail brand blindsided by a sudden shift in consumer preferences.

- Failure to Adapt to Technology: - for example, A legacy business struggling to integrate digital solutions in a tech-driven market.

- Susceptibility to Legal Risks: - for example A startup facing legal challenges due to non-compliance issues.

Professional Intervention:

A Risk management specialist can administer a resilience booster, fortifying the business against potential threats.

5. Chronic Identity Crisis: An Existential Dilemma

Just as an individual grapples with identity crises, a business facing an identity dilemma lacks a clear brand image and market positioning.

Symptoms:

- Inconsistent Brand Messaging: - for example A multinational corporation with disjointed brand messages across regions.

- Failure to Resonate with Demographics: - for example, A tech startup struggling to connect with its target audience due to unclear messaging.

- Frequent Rebranding Without Strategy: - for example A consumer goods company undergoing multiple rebrands without achieving brand clarity.

Professional Intervention:

A Branding expert can perform a brand MRI (Market Responsiveness Index), diagnosing inconsistencies and prescribing a cohesive identity treatment.

6. Ethical Erosion: The Corporate Moral Compass

An erosion of ethics in a business mirrors an individual's deviation from moral principles, leading to reputational damage.

Symptoms:

- Reports of Unethical Behavior: - for example: Whistleblower allegations of corrupt practices within a financial institution.

- Breaches of Ethical Standards: - for example A pharmaceutical company facing public scrutiny for compromising drug safety standards.

- Declining Customer Trust: - for example An e-commerce giant losing customer trust due to data privacy violations.

Professional Intervention:

Ethics and compliance specialists can administer an ethical alignment, restoring integrity and public trust.

7. Financial Indigestion: Operational Upset

In the same way, digestive issues indicate a health problem, financial indigestion in a business reflects mismanagement of financial resources and inefficient operational processes.

Symptoms:

- Uncontrolled Expenses: - for example A hospitality chain grappling with soaring operating costs.

- Poor Inventory Management: - for example A manufacturing company experiencing stockouts and overstock issues.

- Delayed Invoicing and Payment Issues: - for example A service-based business facing cash flow challenges due to delayed client payments.

Professional Intervention:

Financial analysts and operations specialists can perform a corporate endoscopy, optimizing processes for smoother financial digestion.

[11]Entrepreneur's Checklist

Starting a business is thrilling, but it's important to plan, execute, and adapt to succeed. This checklist is a comprehensive guide that covers all aspects of entrepreneurship, from generating ideas to achieving growth. Use it to ensure that you're taking all the necessary steps to build and maintain a prosperous business.

Ideation and Planning:

1. **Identify Your Passion and Strengths**: - What are your interests and strengths that can be translated into a viable business idea?

2. **Market Research**: - Conduct thorough research on your target market, competitors, and industry trends.

---

[11] Let this be your step by step guide

3. **Problem-Solution Fit**: - Clearly define the problem your business solves and ensure there is a demand for your solution.

4. **Business Model Canvas**: - Develop a comprehensive business model canvas outlining key elements like value proposition, customer segments, and revenue streams.

Legal and Compliance:

5. **Business Structure**: - Choose the appropriate legal structure for your business (e.g., sole proprietorship, LLC, corporation) considering liability, taxes, and ownership.

6. **Business Registration**: - Register your business with the relevant authorities and obtain any necessary licenses or permits.

7. **Intellectual Property Protection:** - Identify and protect your intellectual property (trademarks, patents, copyrights) to safeguard your unique offerings.

Financial Management:

8. **Budget and Financial Projections**: - Create a detailed budget and financial projections to understand your cash flow and financial needs.

9. **Funding Options**: - Explore funding options such as personal savings, loans, investors, or crowdfunding based on your business model and growth plans.

10. **Accounting Systems**: - Implement an accounting system to track expenses, and revenues, and maintain financial transparency.

Branding and Marketing:

11. **Brand Identity:** - Develop a strong brand identity, including a memorable logo, consistent visuals, and a compelling brand story.

12. **Online Presence**: - Establish a robust online presence with a professional website, social media profiles, and engaging content.

13. **Target Audience Definition**: - Clearly define your target audience and tailor your marketing strategies to resonate with them.

14. **Marketing Plan**: - Create a comprehensive marketing plan outlining channels, campaigns, and strategies to reach and engage your audience.

Operations and Logistics:

15. **Supply Chain Management**: - Establish an efficient supply chain to ensure timely procurement and delivery of goods or services.

16. **Technology Infrastructure**: - Invest in the necessary technology and software to streamline operations and enhance efficiency.

17. **Team Building**: - Assemble a skilled and motivated team, clearly defining roles and fostering a positive work culture.

Growth and Adaptability:

18. **Scaling Strategies**: - Plan for scalability by identifying growth opportunities, diversification, or expansion strategies.

19. **Customer Feedback Mechanism**: - Implement systems for collecting and analyzing customer feedback to continuously improve your offerings.

20. **Adaptability and Innovation**: - Stay abreast of industry trends, and technology advancements, and be open to innovation for sustained relevance and growth.

Business Plan

A [12]business plan serves as a navigational compass for entrepreneurs and business leaders. It is not just a set of guidelines; it is a strategic masterpiece meticulously crafted to chart the course of a business. Besides internal use, a well-crafted business plan is a powerful tool, instrumental in attracting investors, securing loans, and persuading stakeholders of the business's viability.

How to Draft a Business Plan

To draft a good business plan, you need to start with the executive summary, akin to a business trailer, encapsulating the essence of the plan, and offering a succinct overview of the business concept, goals, and strategies. In **the** business description section, the business's identity is unveiled, including its mission, vision, and the specific problem or need it addresses in the market.

---

[12] This is your customized map of how you will manage your business, thus don`t copy paste other people's business plan.

Market Analysis, a thorough examination of the industry, target market, competition, and market trends are conducted, providing a strategic understanding of opportunities and challenges. The organizational structure segment defines the organizational architecture, spotlighting key team members, their roles, and responsibilities, showcasing the capability to execute the plan.

The products or Services segment has a detailed exposition of the offerings, highlighting unique selling propositions and elucidating how these products or services cater to customer needs. In Marketing and Sales Strategy, the plan articulates robust plans for reaching the target audience, elucidating marketing and sales strategies aimed at achieving business goals.

The operational Plan outlines the day-to-day operations, production processes, technology requirements, and key suppliers are detailed, providing a blueprint for seamless business functioning. The Financial Projections segment outlines comprehensive financial forecasts, encompassing income statements, balance sheets, cash flow projections, and break-even analysis, offering a roadmap to financial success.

Second, lastly, you can include a Funding Request if applicable. If external funding is sought, this section specifies the amount required, its purpose, and the anticipated returns for potential investors or lenders. Last but not least the risk analysis segment should outline all potential risks and challenges are identified, and strategies for risk mitigation are proposed, showcasing a proactive approach to uncertainties.

Benefits of a Business Plan

1. The business plan serves as a clear lens, helping owners articulate and refine their vision, goals, and strategies.

2. It provides a structured framework for making informed, strategic decisions and adapting strategies as needed in a dynamic business landscape.

3. The business plan serves as a compelling narrative, attracting external funding by vividly illustrating the business's potential for success.

4. It functions as a daily guide, ensuring that operational activities align with overarching business objectives and strategies.

5. The plan facilitates proactive identification and mitigation of potential risks, fostering resilience in the face of challenges.

Factors to Consider When Drafting a Business Plan

1. You should customize your business plan to suit its intended audience, whether it be investors, lenders, or internal stakeholders, ensuring relevance and engagement.

2. Ground financial projections and goals in reality by conducting thorough market research and analysis.

3. It's important to use clear and concise language when creating a plan to ensure that it is understandable to people with different backgrounds and levels of knowledge.

4. Recognize the dynamic nature of business environments and regularly update the plan to reflect changes in the industry, market trends, and internal operations.

Features of a Good Business Plan

1. A successful business plan outlines a realistic and feasible roadmap based on thorough market analysis, competition evaluation, and internal capabilities.

2. It strikes a balance between visionary goals and achievable strategies, showcasing ambition tempered by practicality.

3. A good business plan integrates a thorough market analysis, competitor evaluation, and a deep understanding of the target audience. This paints a comprehensive picture of the business landscape.

4. Every aspect of the plan is aligned with the business's objectives and mission, ensuring cohesion in strategic direction.

5. A business plan is not a fixed document but a flexible tool that adapts to the growth of the business. To create a comprehensive and successful business plan, a strategic approach is necessary. Additionally, the plan requires thorough research and a commitment to clear and realistic goal setting. A well-designed

business plan not only guides the business but also instills confidence in stakeholders about the potential for success. It should be presented in a professional, well-organized, and visually appealing manner to enhance its impact and credibility.

[13]Market Entry Strategies

1. Exporting:

When to Use: Exporting is suitable for businesses looking to dip their toes into international markets with relatively low upfront investment.

How it Works: For instance, a small clothing brand based in Kenya may start by exporting its products to online marketplaces in South Africa to gauge customer interest before making a significant investment.

2. Licensing and Franchising:

When to Use: Appropriate for businesses with established brands and standardized business models.

How it Works: An example is McDonald's using franchising to expand globally. Local entrepreneurs pay fees and royalties to operate under the McDonald's brand and benefit from its proven system.

---

[13] Choose the one that works for you.

3. Strategic Alliances and Partnerships:

When to Use: Ideal when entering a market that requires local expertise or distribution channels.

How it Works: For instance, a technology company in Kenya may form a strategic alliance with local universities to navigate cultural nuances and leverage established connections.

4. Joint Ventures:

When to Use: Useful when sharing risks and costs with a local partner and makes strategic sense.

How it Works: An automotive manufacturer from the USA might form a joint venture with a Chinese company to produce and sell cars in the Chinese market, combining their respective strengths.

5. Wholly Owned Subsidiaries:

When to Use: Suitable for businesses with substantial resources and a commitment to full control.

How it Works: Apple establishes wholly owned subsidiaries in various countries to manage its retail stores, maintaining complete control over operations and brand consistency.

6. Direct Investment:

When to Use: Effective for companies with significant financial resources and a long-term commitment.

How it Works: For example, Toyota established manufacturing plants in the United States to meet local demand and reduce production costs.

7. E-commerce and Online Presence:

When to Use: Perfect for businesses with digital products or services that can be easily delivered online.

How it Works: Amazon, originally a U.S.-based online bookstore, expanded globally by leveraging its e-commerce platform to serve customers worldwide.

8. Strategic Acquisitions:

When to Use: Applicability when entering a market quickly is crucial.

How it Works: Facebook's acquisition of Instagram allowed it to swiftly gain traction in the mobile photo-sharing market, accelerating its international growth.

9. Product Adaptation and Localization:

When to Use: Necessary when products or services need customization for local markets.

How it Works: Coca-Cola adapts its marketing and product formulas to cater to local tastes, resulting in unique beverage offerings in different countries.

10. Government Partnerships and Incentives:

When to Use: Relevant when government support is available for foreign businesses.

How it Works: Singapore offers various incentives, including tax breaks and grants, to attract foreign businesses and promote economic growth.

Key Considerations for Choosing a Market Entry Strategy:

1. Assessing the business's risk appetite and capacity to handle potential challenges is crucial for example, a startup might opt for a less capital-intensive strategy to minimize financial risks.

2. Consider the availability of financial, human, and technological resources when choosing a strategy. A tech company may opt for joint ventures to share development costs.

3. Market knowledge is essential. It involves an in-depth understanding of the target market. This includes cultural nuances, regulations, and consumer behavior. For instance, a fashion brand may customize its designs based on cultural preferences.

4. When choosing a strategy, it's helpful to evaluate the level of competition. Also, consider the business's ability to stand out. A technology company might choose strategic alliances to access a partner's established customer base.

5. Long-Term Goals: Aligning the chosen strategy with the long-term goals and vision of the business is critical. An eco-friendly company might prioritize wholly-owned subsidiaries. This ensures sustainability practices are consistently implemented.

6. Flexibility is important: Choosing a strategy that allows for adaptation to changing market conditions ensures resilience. For

example, a software company might initially use exporting but shift to direct investment as it establishes a stronger market presence.

[14]Further Reading Recommendations

To ensure your reading doesn't stop here, here is a list of read-worthy books I highly recommend. I am including as many books as possible. They cover Productivity, business strategy, Marketing, Leadership, product development, startup, self-help, and management. If one topic doesn't appeal to you, you can choose another.

(Top 100 Books)

1. The Blue Ocean Strategy by professors W. Chan Kim and Renée Mauborgne
2. The E Myth by Michael E. Gerger
3. Laws of Succes by Napoleon Hill
4. Good Strategy Bad Strategy by Richard P. Rumelt
5. The Lean Startup by Eric Ries
6. Barbarians to Bureaucrats Corporate Life Cycle Strategies by Lawrence M. Miller
7. Zero to One by Peter Thiel
8. The happiness Hypothesis by Jonathan Hardt

---

[14] Enjoy!!! Bonus recommendation: Chicken Soup for The Soul By Jack Canfield and Mark Victor Hansen

9. The 33 Strategies of War by Robert Greene

10. Mastery by Robert Greene

11. The 48 Laws of Power by Robert Greene

12. The Start-Up J Curve by Howard Love

13. The Mom Test by Rob Fitzpatrick

14. Understanding Michael Porter by Joan Magretta

15. Never Split the Difference by Chris Voss

16. The Atomic Habits by James Clear

17. The Hard Thing About Hard Things by Ben Horowitz

18. Traction By Gabriel Weinberg and Justin Mares

19. Crucial Conversations Tools for talking when stakes are high by Kerry Patterson, Joseph Grenny, Bon McMillan, and Al Switzer

20. The Innovator's Dilemma by Clayton M. Christensen

21. Crossing the Chasm by Geoffrey A. Moore

22. Good to Great by Jim Collins

23. Hooked by Nir Eyal

24. The Great Business Teams by Howard M. Guttman

25. Digital Minimalism by Cal Newport

26. Friction by Roger Dooley

27. Marketing Made Simple by Donald Miller

28. Contagious By Jonah Berger

29. The Subtle Art of Not Giving a Fuck by Mark Manson

30. The 22 Immutable Laws of Marketing by Al Ries and Jack Trout
31. Hacking Growth by Sean Ellis and Morgan Brown
32. This is Marketing by Seth Godin
33. Brand Gap by Marty Neumeier
34. Ultra learning By Scott H Young
35. Power Vs. Force by Dr. David R. Hawkins
36. The Making of Manager by Julie Zhuo
37. They Ask You Answer by Marcus Sheridan
38. The Dichotomy of Leadership by Jocko Willink and Leif Babin
39. Chatter by Ethan Kross
40. Building a Story Brand by Donald Miller
41. Perennial Seller by Ryan Holiday
42. Who by Geoff Smart and Randy Street
43. Influence: The Psychology of Persuasion by Dr. Robert Cialdini
44. The Language of Trust by Michael Maslansky
45. Sprint By Jakes Knapp
46. Flow by Mihaly Csikszentmihalyi
47. Essentialism By Greg Mckeown
48. I will teach you to be Rich by Remit Sethi
49. Thinking Fast and Slow by Daniel Kahneman
50. Who Not How by Dr. Benjamin Hardy and Dan Sullivan

51. The Coaching Habit by Michael Bungay Stanier

52. Start With Why by Simon Sinek

53. Leaders Eat Last by Simon Sinek

54. The Infinite Game by Simon Sinek

55. So Good that they can`t Ignore you, Cal Newport

56. Multipliers by Liz Wiseman

57. Start at The End by Matt Wallaert

58. The Hypomanic Edge

59. Measure What Matter by John Doerr

60. First Break All the Rules by Marcus Buckingham

61. The One Thing by Gary Keller

62. Future Proof by Kevin Roose

63. Your Brain at Work by David Rock

64. The Essence of Success

65. Mindset by Dr. Carol S. Dweck

66. The Unfair Advantage by Ash Ali and Hasan Kubba

67. Think and Grow Rich by Napoleon Hill

68. Breaking the Habit of Being Yourself by Joe Dispenza

69. How to Win Friends and Influence People by Dale Carnegie

70. The Winner Effect by Ian Robertson

71. Unscripted by MJ DeMarco

72. The Psychology of Money by Morgan Housel

73. The Magic of Thinking Big by Dr. David Schwartz

74. 7 Habits of Highly Effective People by Steve Covey

75. The 12 Week Yeah by Brian Moran

76. Steal Like an Artist by Austin Kleon

77. The Little Book of Common-Sense Investing by John C. Bogle

78. Breakthrough Advertising by Eugene M.

79. Pitch Anything by Oren Klaff

80. The Art of getting things done by David Allen

81. Rich Dad Poor Dad by Robert Kiyosaki

82. Cashflow Quadrant by Robert Kiyosaki

83. The Intelligent Investor by Benjamin Graham

84. The Compound Effect

85. Disrupt You

86. Oversubscribed

87. The 4 Hour Work Week

88. The Changing World Order

89. One Up on The Wall Street by Peter Lynch

90. Business Adventures by John Brooks

91. Profit First by Mike Michalowicz

92. Common Stocks and Uncommon Profits by Philip A. Fisher

93. The Fourth Turning by William Strauss and Neil Howe

94. Where are the Customer's Yachts? By Fred Schwed`s

95. Essays In Persuasion by John Maynard Keynes

96. The Clash of the Cultures investment vs speculation by John C. Bogle

97. Dream Big by Cristiane Correa

98. Poor Charlie`s Almanack by Charles T. Munger

99. The Most Important Thing by Howard Marks

100.   The Outsiders by William N. Thorndike. Jr

References

- Kim, W. C., & Mauborgne, R. (2005). Blue ocean strategy: Creating uncontested market space and making the competition irrelevant. Harvard Business Press.

- Gerber, M. E. (2004). The E Myth Revisited: Why most small businesses don't work and what to do about it. Harper Business.

- Hill, N. (1928). Laws of success (new and revised ed.). The Ralston Society Press.

- Rumelt, R. P. (2011). Good strategy/lousy strategy: The difference and why it matters. Crown Business.

- Ries, E. (2011). The lean startup: How today's entrepreneurs use continuous innovation to create radically successful businesses. Crown Business.

- Miller, L. M. (1982). Barbarians to bureaucrats: Corporate life cycle strategies. Harper & Row.

- Thiel, P. A. (2014). Zero to one: Notes on startups or how to build the future. Crown Business.

- Horowitz, B. (2014). The tricky thing about hard things is building a business without easy answers. HarperCollins.

- Weinberg, G., & Mares, J. (2007). Traction: Get a grip on your business. Crown Business.

- Patterson, K., Grenny, J., McMillan, R., & Switzer, S. (2012). Crucial conversations: Tools for talking when stakes are high. Crown Business.
- Christensen, C. M. (1997). The innovator's dilemma: When new technologies cause significant firms to fail. Harper Business.
- Moore, G. A. (1991). Crossing the chasm: Marketing and selling high-tech products to mainstream customers. Harper Business.
- Collins, J. (2001). Good to great: Why some companies leap and others don't. Harper Business.
- Guttman, H. M. (2011). The great business teams: How they work and how you can build one. Jossey Bass.
  Miller, D. (2012). Marketing made simple: A step-by-step guide for small businesses. Harper Business.
- Berger, J. (2013). Contagious: Why things catch on. Simon & Schuster.
- Ries, A., & Trout, J. (1993). The 22 immutable laws of marketing: Violate them at your own risk. HarperCollins.
- Ellis, S., & Brown, M. (2017). Hacking growth: The search for a repeatable process for moving startups from zero to one. Wiley.
- Godin, S. (2007). This is marketing. The Free Press.

APPENDIX: A-

10 ENTREPRENEURSHIP COMMANDMENTS

As you go about your Entrepreneurship Journey, I would like to give you the following 10 commandments, these commandments will keep you and guarantee success when followed faithfully.

1) You must have a Vision.
2) You will not start any business without a good name.
3) Have a business location either Virtually or Physically or both
4) Conduct proper market research
5) Be flexible and adaptable to change
6) Understand the market needs/ demands
7) Have a mentor/coach
8) Do proper accounting
9) Get the right skill and hire right
10) Trust in God always

APPENDIX: B-

TEMPLATES

Executive Summary

Business Name:

Provide the name of your business.

Business Concept:

Briefly describe the nature of your business, its mission, and its vision.

Founding Date:

Specify when the business was established.

Founder(s) and Leadership:

List the key founders and leaders of the business.

Business Description

Industry:

Identify the industry in which your business operates.

Mission Statement:

Define the purpose and core values of your business.

Vision Statement:

Outline your business's long-term aspirations.

Problem/Need:

Explain the problem or need your business addresses in the market.

Market Analysis

Target Market:

Describe your ideal customer or client base.

Competitive Landscape:

Provide an overview of your competitors and their strengths and weaknesses.

Market Trends:

Highlight current and emerging trends in your industry.

Organizational Structure

Legal Structure:

Specify your business's legal structure (e.g., LLC, corporation).

Key Team Members:

List the key members of your team, their roles, and responsibilities.

Products or Services

Offerings:

Detail the products or services your business provides.

Unique Selling Proposition (USP):

Explain what sets your offerings apart from the competition.

Marketing and Sales Strategy

Target Audience:

Define your primary customer demographic.

Marketing Channels:

Outline the channels through which you will promote your business (e.g., social media, content marketing).

Sales Tactics:

Describe the strategies you will use to convert leads into customers.

Operational Plan

Production/Service Delivery:

Explain how your products or services will be produced or delivered.

Technology Requirements:

Specify any technology or tools crucial for your operations.

Supply Chain:

Describe your supply chain and key suppliers.

Financial Projections

Revenue Streams:

Detail your sources of revenue.

Cost Structure:

Outline your fixed and variable costs.

Financial Forecasts:

Provide projections for income statements, balance sheets, and cash flow.

Funding Request (if applicable)

Funding Amount:

Specify the amount of funding you are seeking.

Use of Funds:

Describe how the funds will be used in your business.

Risk Analysis

Identified Risks:

List potential risks your business may face.

Mitigation Strategies:

Outline strategies to mitigate or manage each identified risk.

NB: *This template is a starting point, and you can customize it further based on the specific needs of your business and industry. Remember to continuously update your business plan as your business evolves and the market changes.*

One-Pager Business Plan Template

Business Snapshot

Business Name:

Provide the name of your business.

Mission:

Concisely state the purpose and values of your business.

Founder(s):

List the key founder(s) of the business.

Business Concept

Value Proposition:

Describe the unique value your business offers to customers.

Problem/Need:

Highlight the specific problem or need your business addresses.

Target Market

Customer Segment:

Identify your primary target audience.

Market Differentiator:

Explain what sets your business apart in the market.

Products/Services

Offerings:

List the key products or services your business provides.

Key Features:

Highlight the distinctive features of your offerings.

Marketing Strategy

Key Message:

Summarize the core message you want to convey to your target audience.

Promotion Channels:

Identify the primary channels for promoting your business (e.g., social media, partnerships).

Revenue Model

Primary Revenue Source:

Specify the main source of revenue for your business.

Pricing Strategy:

Outline your pricing strategy.

Key Metrics

Performance Indicators:

Identify key metrics to measure the success of your business (e.g., customer acquisition cost, conversion rate).

Financial Snapshot

Current Revenue (if applicable):

Provide the current revenue figures.

Funding Requirement (if applicable):

Specify any funding needs and the purpose of the funds.

Contact Information

Contact Person:

Provide the name and contact information of the person to reach for inquiries.

Website/URL:

Include your business website or relevant online presence.

NB: *This one-pager business plan template is designed to be a quick reference document that captures the essence of your business strategy. Keep the content clear, concise, and focused on the key elements that will make your business stand out. Adjust the template as needed based on your specific business model and goals.*

A one-page business plan is a concise document that captures the essential elements of your business strategy.

Business Proposal for Funding Template

Executive Summary

Business Name:

Provide the name of your business.

Founder(s) and Leadership:

List the key founders and leaders of the business.

Mission:

Summarize the mission and objectives of your business.

Funding Amount Requested:

Specify the amount of funding you are seeking.

Business Overview

Introduction:

Introduce your business, its core values, and the problem or need it addresses in the market.

Unique Value Proposition:

Highlight the unique value your business brings to customers and how it differentiates itself from competitors.

Market Opportunity

Target Market:

Describe your target market, including demographics and psychographics.

Market Size and Trends:

Provide data on the size of your target market and current trends.

Products/Services

Offerings:

Detail the products or services your business provides.

Key Features:

Highlight distinctive features or competitive advantages.

Marketing and Sales Strategy

Customer Acquisition:

Outline strategies for acquiring and retaining customers.

Sales Channels:

Describe the channels through which you will sell your products or services.

Financial Projections

Revenue Model:

Explain your primary sources of revenue and pricing strategy.

Financial Projections:

Provide forecasts for income statements, balance sheets, and cash flow.

Use of Funds

Allocation of Funds:

Specify how the requested funds will be allocated, including budget breakdown.

Impact on Business Growth:

Explain how the funding will contribute to the growth and success of your business.

Risk Analysis

Identified Risks:

List potential risks your business may face.

Mitigation Strategies:

Outline strategies to mitigate or manage each identified risk.

About the Founder(s)

Background and Experience:

Provide a brief background of the founder(s) and their relevant experience.

Conclusion

Call to Action:

Encourage potential investors to join you in your business journey and express gratitude for their consideration.

NB: *This business proposal serves as a foundation for communicating your business vision, strategy, and financial needs to potential investors. Customize it to fit your specific business model, industry, and funding requirements. Remember to present a compelling case for why your business is a worthy investment, emphasizing both the potential returns and the measures in place to mitigate risks.*

SWOT Analysis Template

Strengths:

1. **Core Competencies:**

- Identify the unique capabilities or resources that give your business a competitive advantage.

2. **Brand Reputation:**

- Highlight the positive perception of your brand in the market.

3. **Skilled Workforce:**

- Recognize the expertise and skills of your team members.

4. **Operational Efficiency:**

- Assess the efficiency of your internal processes and operations.

5. **Innovative Products/Services:**

- List any innovative or unique offerings that set your business apart.

Weaknesses:

1. Limited Resources:
- Acknowledge any constraints in terms of financial, human, or technological resources.

2. Skills Gap:
- Identify areas where your team may lack specific skills or expertise.

3. Operational Challenges:
- Recognize any internal processes that may be hindering optimal performance.

4. Brand Perception:
- Acknowledge any negative perceptions or challenges your brand may face.

5. Dependency on Key Personnel:
- Assess whether the business relies heavily on specific individuals.

Opportunities:

1. Market Trends:
- Identify emerging trends in your industry that your business can capitalize on.

2. Technology Advancements:
- Explore how advancements in technology could benefit your business.

3. New Market Segments:

 - Identify untapped customer segments that could be targeted.

4. Strategic Partnerships:

 - Explore potential collaborations or partnerships that could benefit your business.

5. Regulatory Changes:

 - Assess whether changes in regulations present opportunities for your business.

Threats:

1. Market Competition:

 - Recognize the competitive landscape and potential threats from rivals.

2. Economic Downturns:

 - Acknowledge the impact of economic downturns on your business.

3. Technological Disruptions:

 - Identify potential threats from rapidly changing technologies.

4. Changing Consumer Behavior:

 - Assess how shifts in consumer preferences may impact your business.

5. Supply Chain Disruptions:

 - Recognize the vulnerabilities in your supply chain that could pose threats.

Actionable Insights:

1. Integration of Strengths and Opportunities:

 - Identify strategies to leverage strengths to capitalize on opportunities.

2. Addressing Weaknesses to Exploit Opportunities:

 - Develop plans to overcome weaknesses to take advantage of identified opportunities.

3. Mitigating Weaknesses against Threats:

 - Devise strategies to address weaknesses that could be exploited by potential threats.

4. Leveraging Strengths against Threats:

 - Develop plans to use your strengths to mitigate potential threats.

5. Continuous Monitoring and Adaptation:

 - Establish a process for regular review and adaptation based on changes in the internal and external environment.

NB: *This SWOT Analysis template provides a structured framework to systematically evaluate and strategize around your business's internal and external factors. Customize it based on the specific needs and context of your business.*

Market Research Template

Section 1: Introduction

Business Overview

1. Business Name:

  - Provide the name of your business.

2. Industry:

  - Specify the industry in which your business operates.

3. Purpose of Market Research:

  - Clearly outline the objectives and goals of your market research.

Section 2: Target Market Analysis

Customer Segmentation

1. Demographics:

  - Identify key demographic factors such as age, gender, income, and location.

2. Psychographics:

  - Understand the psychographic traits, values, and lifestyles of your target audience.

3. Behavioral Characteristics:

  - Analyze buying behavior, preferences, and product usage patterns.

Market Size and Growth

1. Current Market Size:

- Estimate the size of your target market.

2. Market Trends:

- Identify current and emerging trends in your industry.

3. Projected Market Growth:

- Predict the expected growth of your market.

Section 3: Competitor Analysis

Competitor Identification

1. List of Competitors:

- Identify direct and indirect competitors.

2. Competitor Strengths:

- Analyze the strengths of your competitors.

3. Competitor Weaknesses:

- Identify the weaknesses of your competitors.

SWOT Analysis (Optional)

1. Strengths:

- Identify your business's internal strengths.

2. Weaknesses:

- Recognize internal weaknesses that may affect your business.

3. Opportunities:

- Explore external opportunities that your business can leverage.

4. Threats:

- Identify external threats that your business may face.

Section 4: Product/Service Analysis

Unique Selling Proposition (USP)

1. USP Definition:

- Clearly define what sets your product or service apart.

2. Key Features:

- List the unique features that make your product or service stand out.

Customer Feedback and Validation

1. Customer Surveys:

- Conduct surveys to gather feedback on your product or service.

2. Testimonials and Reviews:

- Collect and analyze customer testimonials and online reviews.

Section 5: Marketing and Sales Strategy

Marketing Channels

1. Online Channels:

- Identify online platforms for marketing.

2. Offline Channels:

- Identify traditional channels for marketing.

Sales Tactics

1. Sales Funnel:

- Define the stages of your sales funnel.

2. Conversion Strategies:

- Identify strategies to convert leads into customers.

Section 6: Conclusion and Action Plan

Summary of Findings

1. Key Insights:

- Summarize the most important findings from your market research.

2. Implications for Business Strategy:

- Discuss how the findings impact your business strategy.

Action Plan

1. Next Steps:

- Outline the specific actions you will take based on your market research.

2. Timeline:

- Define a timeline for implementing the proposed actions.

NB: *This comprehensive market research template provides a structured framework for entrepreneurs to gather and analyze* *information crucial for making informed business decisions. Customize it based on your specific industry, business model, and research goals.*

www.ingramcontent.com/pod-product-compliance
Lightning Source LLC
Chambersburg PA
CBHW071039290526
45795CB00004B/1229